Broken to Beautiful

A journey towards wholeness, healing and transformation

Shveta Kapur

BlueRose ONE.com DIY
Stories Matter
NewDelhi • London

BLUEROSE PUBLISHERS
India | U.K.

BlueRose ONE.com DIY
Stories Matter
NewDelhi • London

For permissions requests or inquiries regarding this publication, please contact:

BLUEROSE PUBLISHERS
www.BlueRoseONE.com
info@bluerosepublishers.com
+91 8882 898 898
+4407342408967

ISBN: 978-93-7139-240-2

First Edition: August 2025

Dedicated to the almighty and many masters who have walked this path and have created treasures of wisdom for all of us.

To all the seekers and believers who choose hope, healing and inner harmony.

My heartfelt gratitude

To my children – Tejasvi and Anantjeet for their unconditional love and acceptance.
To my husband, for his constant support and encouragement throughout this journey.
To my parents, for sowing the seeds of resilience, empathy and unwavering commitment towards life.

Note for my readers

Thank you for choosing this book. I hope that reading this work brings the shift that you are seeking in your life. If fears hold you back, read the poem given on the next page. As you read, my wish for you-

May you gather the strength to return to your wholeness!

May you shine through your brokenness!

With grace and gratitude, may you grow manifolds!

(Pro-tip- Use the blank spaces to make notes, write or draw to engage more and personalize your journey).

FEAR By Kahlil Gibran

It is said that before entering the sea
a river trembles with fear.

She looks back at the path she has travelled,
from the peaks of the mountains,
the long winding road crossing forests and villages.

And in front of her,
she sees an ocean so vast,
that to enter
there seems nothing more than to disappear forever.

But there is no other way.
The river cannot go back.

Nobody can go back.
To go back is impossible in existence.

The river needs to take the risk
of entering the ocean
because only then will fear disappear,
because that's where the river will know
it's not about disappearing into the ocean,
but of becoming the ocean.

CONTENTS

Praise for the Author

Shveta has been a passionate educator to the core, for almost two decades.

The honesty that she brings along with her persona, has helped her triumph the turbulence of her professional and personal life. The best part is - she has carved Diamonds out of her pebbles (this book being one of those gems).

May this book be of help to those in need and may it uplift all.

My best wishes to the author.

-Shailender

INTRODUCTION

"If everything around seems dark,
look again, you may be the light."-
Rumi

Embracing the beauty of brokenness

Brokenness - not a failure but a passage to Self-discovery

A seed breaks inside the earth and then emerges as a fresh tender sapling with the potential to reach its fullest form to bloom in its beauty!

Imagine if that first breaking wouldn't have happened. Nature is the greatest teacher…

Breaking opens us for expansion.

Breaking happens as part of life, so embrace it.

That perspective is where our choice as human beings lie and what truly matters is how we see ourselves - broken to be better or broken to be bitter.

In human experience, breaking is an unwanted event because of the tough feelings like pain, loss, failure and sadness associated with it. But emotions come in full bundle- love and loss, joy and pain, success and failure etc.

In our society, there is a constant narrative to bind people without much thought about finding beauty in relationships. We all continue living these bonds without trying to acknowledge and address the internal breaking that happens slowly, over the years, creating distances in our very own relationships.

We learn to champion masking and hiding our inner breaking, missing the opportunity for rediscovery and living a life of fulfilment and purpose. Each of us are like those seeds with potent energy.

Imagine if the seed resists breaking, will it grow?

Perhaps, we are conditioned to believe that breaking makes things less valuable and we often find ourselves, showing bin to things that break instead of restoring or repairing by filling up the cracks or rearranging the pieces.

Much like relationships in the present times; formed for bonding but result in breaking, falling apart and left to starve without much attention to explore the hidden opportunity.

My journey into breaking gave me an opportunity to birth a newer version of me, much like an egg which breaks open as life, only when the chick is ready from the inside, to face the outer world.

Together, let's see our Brokenness as an opportunity to find fresh avenues for cultivating love, peace, compassion and empathy. Healing ourselves need patience and time but it surely is worth a journey to begin.

When I felt broken, I was pained, I felt

shattered as I didn't know what to do with it. No one had taught me how to deal with this brokenness within me, yet I felt it deep within my heart and was also clueless on finding the root cause, forget doing something about it.

In my head, I thought that it's normal and happens with everybody so, I never went deep into the pains that my body was signaling since ages. Many of us keep living in this state of blind acceptance. Eventually, this became my own drift up view of life and limited me in my relationships.

<u>Pause and reflect-</u> What does your view of life look like?

I have come to realize that nothing breaks in a day; it starts with small cracks, which we miss, resulting in the shattering; and this unaddressed breaking emerges strongly, demanding our time and attention. Experiencing this kind of damage is catastrophic.

For a long time, I followed the narratives about life and relationships and kept looking for fixes by eating medicine, thinking good, reading positive thoughts and moving on with life, as usual.

Kept going.

Kept strolling and crawling and sprinting but won't stop and acknowledge the invitation that my brokenness was asking me to process for the deeper, internal exploration of myself. *(as I see this now)*

It was certainly unusual and I suddenly wanted to scan people with similar breaking experience but didn't find anyone like me. At that time, I couldn't recognize that '*All pots don't break the same way*', so all of us have our own internal breaking, calling from the depths of our hearts to address the core and discover ourselves, that may not be visible outside.

One of the most manipulated lessons I find is that - *Time heals everything.* Yes, it does but nothing can substitute a timely action emerging from kind attention to our own brokenness. This makes me wonder how this valuable lesson is half understood. Relying on this thought creates a belief that robs our own agency of doing something to improvise or prevent further breaking of self and relationships leading to increased stress and trauma through the continued micro moments of intense pain.

Another beautiful lesson that I learnt to deconstruct is— *'Do your karma but don't try to control the outcome'*. It simply means, keep taking your actions with care and consistency but don't run for results.

This means that – 'Our power lies in taking timely action!'

In my experience, much more breaking happened in my pursuit to chase life and relationships...there was an awkward ignorance of internal brokenness that was felt in silence but my attention was all flowing towards controlling the outcomes in the external reality.

This kind of living is like a mirage in the desert!

I lived there once, but not anymore.

GRATITUDE LETTER TO MYSELF

Dear Shveta,

I want to thank you for the love you have brought in yourself and that same love is radiating upon all those around you.

You are one of those special people that the universe has chosen to heal lives, touch lives and transform lives with gentleness, compassion and empathy.

You have chosen the path towards wholeness. This way of being has helped you heal and rediscover your own self and your relationships.

It's been a messy and muddling journey but with strength, faith and inner belief, you have learnt to lead the inside out transformation- so authentic and pure.

May love, joy and peace be with you. The universe is guiding and I love how you choose to surrender to a higher power without wanting to control the outcome yet trying to reach your goals.

Trust and kindness in your heart – your biggest strengths.

'Being okay with not being okay' is one of your greatest

learnings too. I am grateful to you for bringing this inner change and shift within your own being.

You give hope to people. You help them navigate the riskier path of finding themselves and living wholesome lives.

Much Love to you for showing courage by sharing your journey and lessons with your readers to empower and enable them to find inner beauty by embracing their own brokenness.

Pause a minute and use the given space to write one short note/ letter to yourself. Illustrate or sketch if you like to.

My journey through pain, healing and transformation

As a child, I had heard people saying pain is a part of life but never could find out the navigation points on –

How to deal with it?

What can one do when lingering pains (physical or emotional) cause internal breaking?

Observing adults around me, thinking about loss and love in life, the mind was just hopeful that those experiences are for people who do something bad or ill for others. Why would my family have to go through any pain?

So, this way I grew up believing that- 'Struggles are a part of life' and keep working, keep toiling and things will get better. Time will heal everything. I wouldn't do bad with anybody in my life, so why would anything bad happen to me?

But as they say, life has its own way of teaching us lessons that come from the most unwanted, ugly and unpleasant experiences. These could be conflict with a loved one, argument with a co-worker, a disagreement with boss, unmet expectations from self, not feeling worthy or enough-etc.

My notion of bad was so limited.

These experiences are not the ones that we consciously choose. These just happen but the learned pattern is to keep going and wishing that one day things will get better. Get your chin up and work towards improvement of self as that's the only thing I could do! Somehow, I always believed in the idea of self-improvement.

Now, when I look back at the previous version of myself, I feel amazed to notice how hopeful I have been amidst the inner chaos that I was going through.

All my ideal notions shattered one by one.

My life before my marriage was different and then after marriage the same me was trying and living the same me. But it wasn't accepted!

BOOM!

I was hit and didn't understand what's going wrong in my life. I had worked hard to study despite challenges at home which was no less than fighting a battle to be better than my situation. I never let the situations take me over and never chose to sit with this belief that this is how life is designed.

I had deep questions:

- What is life?
- Why do things happen the way they happen?

I am good, not harming anybody then what's not being done right. This inner dialogue had initiated in my early 20's.

I was a young lass growing up with dreams of love and forming deep, long-lasting relationships.

My mother has been my strength and was always the one I looked up to.

I remember reading this quote on television by Late Mother Teresa – "I know God will not give me anything I can't handle. I just wish He didn't trust me so much."

These words gave me strength and made me

feel that I am a trusted child of God. Therefore, despite our financial struggles, I stayed hopeful by navigating the path with acceptance, not complaints. After all, this quote also meant that God believes that I am strong, so I must keep going, come what may!

In 2022 after COVID-19, my body broke down and I faced multiple health issues. This just disintegrated everything within me.

Intense pain and unacknowledged grief led me towards healing and transformation. The body didn't collapse in a day. It just accumulated each unprocessed feeling and kept it close as pains and aches. I realized that my relationship with internal pain and breaking had been long. The very pain that I never imagined to be living with was my ally since 2007-2008. Only the form of pain and the intensity kept changing for years.

I never could acknowledge that this as a deep opportunity to learn and cultivate awareness of my own self and my own thought patterns.

Looking back, I realize that my own beliefs and value system created bigger walls and wells within me and my relationships.

I was missing on learning to accept and explore the depths of my own mental, emotional, physical and psychological pains and dilemmas. My only solution to everything was to fix it by eating medicine, some temporary exercise, giving in to sugar cravings and then, keep going!

No time to stop and share!

No time to pause to listen to my body and attend to the pains.

At 26, I gave birth to my first child. She held

me tight and kept me anchored during my emotionally challenging and mentally exhausting times. Throughout this experience of pregnancy, I was happy yet deeply saddened by the multitude of events and situations beyond my control. At that time, I felt deep within me that the only priority is to have a safe and healthy delivery.

In this phase, I always wondered:

- Why isn't this phase of my life joyful like everybody else's?
- Why others were seemingly numb to what a woman goes through in this phase of her life?

I did not know how to manage my emotions back then. I just thought that time will heal everything for me and my situations will improve.

At 28, my second child was born. This pregnancy had a few complications right from the beginning and my body stayed in a state of unease and chronic conditions like acute constipation and severe backache, which subsided temporarily but kept re-occurring in various forms and intensities, and resulted in frequent visits to the doctor. Some years ago, a great family split had happened and I was quickly reminded of some scenes of the famous Bollywood movie – 'Deewar'.

At that point, I made a silent choice that this is not going to be my battle at all because I had dreams of my own and I kept hopes alive for myself and my children.

Being an independent, powerful and supporting partner, who contributes before demanding, always mattered to me. That's the idea of a girl who wants a loving and long-lasting relationship without compromising on her own autonomy, voice, and agency in the way we live our lives as a family.

I never believed in the concept of self-sacrifice and forced adjustments and the glory that the world attaches to these highly popularized values, especially for women. Instead, I believed in the ideals of co-existence, co-regulation, and companionship.

Again, nothing turned out as I had planned it to be.

Interestingly, as young girls we all get shaped by the widespread notions around love, marriage and careers. I wonder why there is an absence of conversation on how we can lead our lives beautifully with so much love, peace and growth in our relationships- in families, with friends, or at work while loving ourselves first and addressing our agony as it arises.

But I had this strange approach- Ignore and move on. Stay positive with your chin up and smile through things as time will heal everything. I proudly offered the same advice to my colleagues or anybody who I thought would need a positive approach towards their lives.

Bickering and cribbing and crying over situations that I cannot control- I carefully stayed away from such behaviors. Being vulnerable and appearing helpless was never my choice.

So, I chose to be happy no matter what and be my own sunshine yet longing to be understood emotionally, was the only vacuum that I felt deeply and I find many people feeling the same in their heart.

What we do in our professional life, also impacts our personal lives. This parallel journey has the power to shift our perceptions and personal values.

From my own experience, I would say that teachers have hard lives as compared to many other professions that I see. This profession demands not only physical but continuous mental, emotional engagement as we are in the service of learning and shaping young minds.

As much as I owe to this profession and each life that I could serve, I can't ignore the fact that this work is exhaustive in nature. The demands for innovation and upskilling for professional growth do take a toll on the overall health and well-being of teachers.

With personal expansion of being a mother, a homemaker, a wife, a daughter, an elder sister, a daughter-in-law, I never gave myself permission to pause and contemplate on the roots of my unending body aches and emotional suffering.

I had learnt that life is both pleasure and pain. So, I kept tossing the coin to pleasure and ignored the pain using a masked belief that I am staying strong, no matter what.

Or

Perhaps, my heart might have tried to whisper that it wants to be cared for, but I didn't know how to bring relief in those stressful situations or conflict between the head and the heart.

Subconsciously, my coping mechanism was to resist spending time processing the tough emotions of anger, grief, sadness and frustration. It can never be that we don't feel such deep emotions but overtime, a conditioned pattern of numbing these emotions gets formed as an adaptive behavior to maintain peace and harmony in the closest relationships. Sometimes, thinking of consequences also prevent us. Discretion is vital here.

Sub-consciously, I was trying to avoid conflict and suppress my own emotional needs as I assumed that no one actually cared or had the capacity to support me at a deeper level, hence no expectations.

However, now I believe that having 'no expectations' is a fallacy and as social beings we all operate through expected experiences in our lives. This keeps us motivated and in action.

The learning is- Embrace your expectations, first from yourself and then from others. Our social interactions are full of expectations! I would say, expect but don't judge if it's not met.

Pause and reflect-Are you aware of your own expectations from yourself? Write any 3 of them.

Back to my story. With those thought patterns, I was stuck in a cycle of recurring pains which were stored as trauma in the body and forced the body to shut down. I stumbled upon a wonderful book titled *'When the body says no' by Dr. Gaber Mate.* Reading this book gave me hope that my suffering can be worked upon and the fact that the brain rewires to form new patterns for a new reality just fascinated me, as I was seeking solutions.

All I needed was to pause, reflect and face my inner self. I had to listen to the whispers of my heart, even if it meant revisiting each experience of my life until that point in time. I made a list of emotions that were attached with various life events of the past.

One of the biggest realizations was that – for the longest time I had experienced sadness, grief and isolation. I was so busy in my own battles of life and wanting, that I reached a stage where I started ignoring and suppressing my own need for authenticity and assertiveness. It was a shocking realization that I had lost my own self somewhere in the journey. It was hard to accept.

Pains of the past bring so much insight that we can use this information to process our pains and make meaning by understanding our own thoughts, behaviors, actions and feelings. I also had a role in that event. It was a choice to stay silent in those turbulent times to maintain order in the surroundings and not to offend anybody.

But now, after COVID 19 in 2022, I needed to create a changed reality for myself, so that there is good health, quality time and belongingness within me.

There is a Buddhist teaching found in the text 'Sallatha Sutta', known as The Arrow. It says that if an arrow hits you, the pain will be there. If a second arrow strikes exactly at the same point on your body, the pain felt will be 10 times greater.

This is much similar to some unwanted events like being rejected, losing something or failing an exam, getting an injury- this is all like the first arrow which certainly causes hurt and pain.

However, the second arrow is fired by **us**, when we react or repeat or stay anxious and not accept the suffering/event. This way we create more pain for ourselves. No amount of regret or lamenting can undo the hurt caused by the first arrow.

Please note that the second arrow can be a little judgement of ourselves, some fear of the future or anger and telling in the mind- “I don't like to be in this pain”, “I don’t deserve this”. It is our mind weaving stories and spirals of unhelpful thoughts and energies. In this situation, we forget that we cannot undo anything of the past but can choose to move forward by accepting the first arrow.

Mindfulness is one of the best practices that allows us to stay with the wound and be aware that suffering is a part of life and there are conscious choices that we always have. We must not keep creating resentment of the past or stay anxious for the unknown future.

Power of Love and Resilience in rebuilding oneself

Practicing love and resilience to repair the broken aspects of myself and my relationships helped in bringing the real transformation that was seeking for me. During this journey, the new belief that I created was that 'What I'm seeking is also seeking me'. Therefore, the only way to approach this situation was to rebuild and rearrange pieces and parts of myself without blaming and being guilty of my own ignorance. I had a strong calling to look beyond the known and discover my truest self, starting with these profound wonderings…

– Who am I?

– What should I do now so that I don't end up creating the same situation for myself again?

The patterns that get repeated in life create

same results, so learn about your patterns and change your life.

I'm glad that I approached the situation with curiosity and patience to let things emerge from within. I chose to stay with the same relationships and not break away from everything that caused painful experiences in the past.

I wanted to fulfil each of my roles and do whatever the responsibilities demand but with awareness and inner resolution to shift the realities of my own life. Starting from the most immediate physical limitation. This time I wanted a deeper cure that heals my life.

Rebuilding requires introspection, contemplation, and a thorough scrutiny to find out -

1. Where are the cracks?

2. How severe has the damage been?
3. What impact has it created on my life?
4. How do I learn to live with the cracks and wounds?
5. Can there be life without cracks and scars?

An Invitation to the Reader:

This book is your guide to wholeness

Read this book with love and gentleness flowing through your heart.

Each sensation or a thought or a feeling that my words trigger in your body and mind- just gently allow these to flow within.

Open yourselves to create a healing space within, that allows you to go into the deeper experiences sitting within your mind, body and spirit.

Make a conscious choice to stay away from any judgements of people, places or events that you read or resonate with.

Choose hope and compassion to be your constant companions in this journey of change and transformation.

Allow the unfolding to flourish within you.

Trust the power of the higher consciousness vibrating within all of us, guiding and protecting us.

Shift your thoughts to shift your energy and attract what your heart truly desires.

Notice if there are any self-sabotaging patterns that you hold within and be brave enough to look at your own follies first without analyzing or judging any experience or emotion attached to it.

Just be an observer and sit with this awareness arising from your journey.

Let your body be your home and keep in touch with the feeling in your body, you might need a conscious effort to practice this.

Strengthen the mind-body connection with

deep breathing practices as you navigate this journey of your own life- finding beauty in brokenness.

Re-read this work as many times as you want and do not try to push a timeframe or impose a deadline to your own healing. Experience a full range of emotions that flow like energy - only changes form but neither created nor destroyed.

Lastly, be in tune with yourself as you move in and out of the sections, illustrations and various chapters of this book.

May this book allow the pure transformative process to begin within you. It has reached you to help you find own greatness and grace.

Honor your own inner knowing and operate from a seeker and a believer's mind.

We are born whole and complete. The healing process is about re-integrating the broken parts of our being and returning to this wholeness as we live with purpose and meaning.

Let love, patience and forgiveness be with all of us.

Thank you for choosing this journey of transformation for yourself!

PART 1

"When you are about to find fault with someone, ask yourself: What fault of mine most nearly resembles the one I am about to criticize?"

---Marcus Aurelius

Understanding brokenness:

The fall and the struggle

Chapter 1

The illusion of Wholeness

Illusion is the first of all pleasures.

-Oscar Wilde

Society's pressure to be "whole"

There are constructs that one needs to navigate in order to be successfully living and to hold a respectable position in society. As a young child growing in the 90's and seeing the Y2K shift, I also nurtured *a certain view of success.* I loved the multinational boom and was charmed by the corporate life that I would often imagine myself embracing in order to live a great life with a great job and eventually a great family of my own. Everything would then be complete and whole, fitting into this picture. So, after my graduation I chose to pursue MBA- the most sought-after qualification to help me get a wonderful job in a reputed MNC, bringing status, money and fame for the family.

As an aspiring corporate employee, I never believed in the narrative that my mother was trying to present before me as an alternative career. According to her, teaching was the best career for girls because it helps one balance both work and life better than any other profession. She herself was a teacher and found joy in her own profession. But that was not enough a reason for me to follow her recommendation.

During my MBA studies and different jobs that I was doing to support my family financially, I learnt about the career break that women in corporate have to take, owing to their duties as the primary caregiver to the child, post marriage. For them, continuing their jobs is harder because of long office hours and sometimes, lesser understanding from their own families to pursue their careers. I had only read such reports and data which kind of scared me as I had a different perception of this job profile. That made me reconsider my options at the age of 21.

This perception became a reality, when during my internship at the HSBC Bank in Noida, I experienced those long working hours which were not at all in sync with the kind of family life I wanted for myself, especially after having children (*I always liked to plan my life and make informed choices)*. I was okay with the work but we were expected to report at 9:30 am without any fixed time to go back home. There was a strange practice of seeking permission, which I never felt is the right practice to follow for the rest of my work life, as this would have a ripple effect on my personal and family life too. I found it a complex way of functioning and too subjective a tradition in the corporate sector- all this was too much for me to bear each day. Those three months of internship helped me make better choices and I was able to rethink about my career in alignment with my expectations from my own life.

As they say, our parents know the best, I shifted my energy towards making a career in Teaching. It started with pursuing Bachelor in Education(B.Ed) and then Masters in English

(M.A.) and a host of other certifications over this successful career spanning almost two decades.

This kind of clarity saved me from any regrets in my career. Moreover, I felt motivated to learn and grow as an individual who is aware of her priorities as well as things that work and a few that don't.

It still holds relevance and keeps me anchored to a few fundamentals when I think of my current professional and personal life.

Continuing the story, I was eager to shift to a career in education and was pleased to have made this transition. Further, marriage happened so things were just going as I planned them to be.

In my understanding, I was sure that I will have:

1. No career break.
2. More time to be available for my children and family.
3. A regular source of income for a decent living.
4. Overall, an improved work-life balance.

This was my world of illusion of wholeness.

I was happy to navigate the world of teaching but in a different manner than my mother. She was working in a government school and I had done my senior school studies in one such school. I loved my school. But as someone who longed for a corporate career, working in such a setup never appealed to me. Mumma kept insisting on trying for government jobs, but I remember rejecting this idea and telling her with dreams of an unknown work life that, "Ma, I don't want to be a Behen ji."

As a cost, I was okay to let go of the stability and secured growth that comes with such jobs. I still see so many people longing for a government job, but strangely I never aspired for it. But like many of us, I also couldn't escape the family's insistence on at least trying, so yes, I tried too but, with a half-hearted attempt and couldn't get through.

In 2007, I got my first full-time teaching assignment and in 2008, I welcomed my first child and life moved on as I planned it to be!

My illusion was short lived! The bumps were waiting to meet me!

Reflect: Are you someone like me, living in your illusions of wholeness? What does it look like for you at present?

Life always has its own plans, messy and muddy but miraculously magical!

How pain and struggle shape our true selves

Pains and struggles have been my biggest teachers and each time I faced a challenge in life, I knew that I had the courage to face it. With this undying belief in me, I always felt that I can find my way through life.

Now, when I reflect back, this approach made me not seek support and hence, I became a lone warrior. I would often encourage myself by thinking in my head and talking to myself-

"What if I don't have any support, even from my own family, So what, if they don't understand me now, some day they will."

Those thoughts invited a pattern that shaped me in my formative years as a young adult and even as a married woman.

I had no way to figure out reasons for this painful, monotonous grind of managing family, with children and a demanding job and confrontations and lingering conflicts arising in the day-to-day life.

I just motivated myself with positive thoughts without sharing my pains and voicing my concerns because I thought it's not that important. Maybe I didn't trust myself enough. The 'Good Girl syndrome' mixed with the 'Never say die' attitude, I kept stumbling and bumping my way, handling all pieces together for the common good of my entire family.

Until Covid-19 hit me in 2022, I had switched four teaching jobs which brought fatigue, pressure and performance anxiety not only for me but my children too. Not all job switch were my choices and need, but each change brought its own opportunities laced with challenges.

The chronic health issue in second half of the year 2022, made me question myself and I had to examine my own approach towards life and relationships. It is important to be with each other, no matter what, maintain silence as that is Golden.

What my heart couldn't express, the body did. My own body, proved my approach wrong because the result was emotional, mental pains laced with guilt, ignorance, non-acceptance and remorse of the lost time and the way I had lived my life, always looking at others' interest first and not being reciprocated the same, it hit even harder.

Running around every role and duty, performing it to my fullest potential, drained me at a personal level. I always averted pain and in fact dismissed it, like many of us. But physical pain had been there since my first pregnancy in 2008. It was a tough time emotionally and made me feel vulnerable each day. The surge of emotions would sweep me over and, in the washroom, I would weep incessantly.

At that stage, I couldn't figure out why this was happening to me. No answers I could ever find and life moved on. I marveled

What made me respond like this?

What is it that I need to pay attention to?

Reflect- Do you have any similar experience to relate to?

In 2025, when I look back, I realize that I ruthlessly ignored my own emotions and feelings. There were early signs of deep pain originating from unresolved conflicts, which unaddressed became trauma, that I was storing in my body unconsciously.

As a Mindfulness coach and SEL trainer, I now know for sure that emotions don't die. They need to be channelized with acceptance and awareness.

Nowhere, growing up in my childhood and even in my adult life, I learnt -

1.What to do with tough and difficult emotions?

2.How to handle when things go worse in our own family dynamics?

3.Is ignoring and leaving the issue unresolved the only way to live life?

I wondered if there was something about life that our elders missed sharing with us.

Past is a lost opportunity but we can understand life only backwards!

I learnt to sit with those whispers which made me feel resentful but opened doors for me to look through the layers of conditioning that each of us are given at homes, in families and even, at school.

Taking full responsibility of my healing journey, I would often feel guilty of inaction and ask myself---

Why didn't I voice my concerns in time?

Why did I leave it for others to understand?

What do I need to learn about my approach towards life?

The interplay of family roles, personal aspirations and motherly duties would often leave me feeling exhausted but I had learnt to look at the bright side of life. Staying positive was a choice I would always make whenever I felt low during the day, especially at home. The demands of time and attention and restrictions that motherhood brought were challenging for me to handle.

At this point, I am deliberately choosing not to shift the narrative to explain what happens in our Indian homes, when there are three generations living in the same home. The big bag of expectations is on the woman and if she works, she will have to keep working harder and harder to pull up and perform in each role– a wife, a daughter-in-law, a mother, a cook, a home- manager, a partner, a teacher etc.

But here I was stuck in a hamster wheel of the daily chores and routines.

The concept of having time for recreation had

taken a solid hit. For me, this was the least important thing at that stage in my life. How about you?

Life kept going, I had learnt to sail with the flow. In my heart, I was hopeful that one day, everybody around me will understand how life's daily situations are creating friction and how with understanding we all can navigate the challenges better, keeping each other's respect and trust intact– too much of an expectation at my end!

In 2010, I delivered my second child. Again, it was a tough time for me as it was a bittersweet moment of pleasure and acute body pains. It restricted my movement and the doctor would say, "This happens." I would tell myself, once the baby is out in the world, everything would be normal.

At 28, I had two young children, a teaching job which was getting harder to manage due to my physical pains because standing, correcting notebooks, running for bus duties, dispersal– all this needed physical strength and agility, which was slowly getting reduced because of various reasons like sleepless nights, not enough rest, not eating properly and not feeling at ease, coupled with strong resistance to protect my own choices and aspirations. The biggest of all- not registering my own emotional needs.

The aches in my legs and sleepless nights again were making things harder, especially when I had to get up early, cook and run to catch the bus. Each day was no less than a battle. With faith in my heart, I kept going without complaining. I would often tell my supervisor at school– "I will for sure show up at work, so no substitutions are needed for me."

The red marks showing late arrival, salary cuts, giving up on two annual appraisals- I never felt that it was an alarming situation to operate in, especially for myself. As long as the job was there, I didn't bother much about all the internal noise and whisperings.

After all, this was a temporary phase and things will get better with time– I would often repeat this in my mind.

So, chin up and keep going– self-talk has helped me during each stage of my life. I would keep visiting the doctor for pains in my lower back, knees, left leg, and neck quite frequently– never stopping to notice what my body was trying to tell me.

As I see in the hindsight, I was never ready to heed to these pains and recognize the roots, forget about doing anything to restore the balance that my body was losing. I was slipping into a state of dis-ease, slowly and gradually over many years- emotionally, mentally and physically.

We must remember that we are one whole- an integration of mental, emotional, social and physical states. Each of the state has the power to impact the other.

Unknowingly I practiced- Disconnection!

Personal Reflection: The moment of realization of my own disconnection

In June 2019, the first time I was shaken when I experienced a physical jolt in my body during one of the reflection sessions. As we were guided to follow the Body scan technique to dig deeper into our own selves, for the first time, I had realized that I had stored the pains in my body.

The emotional pains of my first pregnancy were sitting within me. It hit me hard to the core. In 2019, almost a decade after my first pregnancy I could still feel the pain which had actually become a trauma, that I could feel so strongly in my body. It was undealt, unprocessed, and unreleased so the body just kept it!

This was the opening that made me reflect that

I want to be aware of my own self. Also, this was a wake-up call to recognize that there are familial conflicts that I must try to resolve with courage and clarity.

Something deeper had struck within during that experience. It felt uncomfortable and tight in my chest. I felt overwhelmed to notice the emergence of this awareness.

This jolt could not be forgotten and I was unhappy, dealing with boils and physical breakdowns, was on medication including muscle relaxants, suppressants and pain reliever for a long time.

That day I realized the meaning of this saying that -Ignorance is bliss! (I couldn't ignore this anymore and hence, the blissful state of illusion in my head was crashing)

The internal pain was powerful and it wanted

to speak to me. The painful memories started playing in my head and the unexpressed pain had emerged stronger than I could even explain to people around me. I didn't know what to do with this kind of feeling.

Surely, I had realized the disconnections and the need to claim my space and time but I needed someone to help me decode this situation and prescribe some actions for me.

It was such a unfathomable, life-changing awareness to sit with. I felt broken and disconnected inside without any visible signs on the outside. I questioned myself-

How could I deceive my own self?

Life moved on. I moved on. But these painful memories aren't moving on. I often thought to myself. Some internal change was needed to change my outside reality.

The hunt was on for an effective mechanism to deal with this situation in my life. I was in the middle of this awareness journey and didn't know how to restore my connection with myself!

We are what we think and feel and do!

Chapter 2

When life breaks you open

"Real knowledge is to know the extent of one's ignorance." – Confucious

The breaking points: Loss, Trauma, Heartbreak and Adversity

As a young aspirational girl, I was tuned to be positive and chirpy all the time. In my understanding, we create our own lives by studying well, growing through challenges and having a great job, get married, have children, and then just enjoy the love that the partner and family members bring to our lives. After all, a family is a unit and the idea is to live and grow together. The fundamental belief was when I am not being bad to anyone– Why would anyone be bad to me? *(I still believe in the goodness that lies in each of us, it just gets layered as we navigate life and keep accumulating or gathering or borrowing beliefs in order to live a good life).*

I have not come across anyone in my life so far who would say/do/act as an evil force or an identified villain like Prem Chopra Ji in Bollywood films. Remembering the antagonist in moral stories, I kept looking for an antagonist in my own life story.

Everybody wants to do well, live well, love well and keeps juggling roles throughout life to achieve this idea of a successful life. But this 'well' isn't defined the same for all. I think everyone's 'well' is different.

However, there are the fundamental markers like studying, marrying, job to earn money and then kids. After this, nobody helps to explore what to strive for and how to live life peacefully and joyfully while dealing with situations and unforeseen struggles.

I wonder who really prepares us for life.

For me also, once these markers were achieved, I didn't know what to achieve next.

Does that mean that there is nothing more left as a checkpoint to tick in life?

I would often wonder–

- What is life?
- Is this what life being all about?

Somewhere deep in my heart I used to feel that there is more to life. After all, in my growing years, I always had something to look forward to and be the hero in my story who faces challenges and emerges stronger.

As I trace back to this thought, I look backwards and can certainly understand how my checkboxes were ticked pretty early in life. I feel grateful for that and have the privilege to look beyond the lessons that were in store for me.

So, my timeline looks like this

0	1982	My arrival on the planet
15-16	1998	Passed X
17-18	2000	Passed XII and started graduation studies + My father's accident
19	2001	My first job at Boston Computer Education

20	2002	My second job
21	2003	Completed graduation + Computer Education + MBA
22	2004	Got engaged
23	2005	Completed my MBA + Interned at HSBC (decided to shift career) + Got married + enrolled in B.Ed
24	2006	B.Ed. course session completion
25	2007	Landed my first teaching job (fulltime, started as a PRT)
26 to 28 (Health issues started at 28)	2008	Had my first child + job + family expectations with care duties Took a 6-month maternity break
	2009	Got back to my teaching job, looking for growth + parenting duties +postpartum

<table>
<tr><td rowspan="2"></td><td></td><td>recovery period</td></tr>
<tr><td>2010</td><td>Had my second child + job + duties at work + expectations at home</td></tr>
<tr><td>29</td><td>2011</td><td rowspan="5"><ul><li>Parenting + job aspiration for growth + no compromise on my work + home duties</li><li>Aging parents to take care</li><li>Financial expectations to build something together i.e. own home</li><li>Desperate to look for another job for progression</li><li>Enrolled in courses and certifications</li></ul></td></tr>
<tr><td>30</td><td>2012</td></tr>
<tr><td>31</td><td>2013</td></tr>
<tr><td>32</td><td>2014</td></tr>
<tr><td>33</td><td>2015</td></tr>
<tr><td>34</td><td>2016</td><td><ul><li>NIEPA</li></ul></td></tr>
</table>

<table>
<tr><td rowspan="3">35 to 37

Emotional health crumbling + disturbances in relationships</td><td>2017</td><td rowspan="3"><ul><li>Job shift to PSG + performance stress + travel fatigue and long hours at work</li><li>money + safety with children- ample food as lunch was available + child study discounts</li></ul>I enjoyed the exhaustion that my job brought because it helped my entire family.</td></tr>
<tr><td>2018</td></tr>
<tr><td>2019</td></tr>
<tr><td>38</td><td>2019-20</td><td><ul><li>Job shift to HXLS + performance stress + travel fatigue and long hours at work</li><li>Car crash</li></ul></td></tr>
<tr><td>39</td><td>2021</td><td><ul><li>Relocated to a new city and a new school. performance stress + COVID time</li></ul></td></tr>
</table>

		• Delta wave- family suffered LOSS • Multiple heath issues
40	2022	• Diagnosed with Rheumatoid Arthritis, physical mobility compromised (left full time job)
New chapter begins through healing	2023 2024 2025	Period of Rapid Transformation- Ultra phase • Learnt my lessons through healing journey personally • Redefined my relationship with myself • Examined my own beliefs + shifted perspectives Reclaimed my wholeness and working to empower others at professional level

Back to the story…

This wasn't the life that I imagined for myself. I didn't do anything bad to anybody. Like all of us, I also repeated this in my head.

There wasn't anyone to blame and I didn't even want to because I knew it's not the way I function in the world. I believe that the ownership and responsibility of **Being or Becoming** lies with me.

I lost myself somewhere, when I tried to fit in and live according to the expectations of others. I lost myself when I gave in for the sake of others' happiness at the cost of my own. I took it as a challenge as I was the most courageous woman I knew of, after my mother.

But despite that--

I lost myself because I ignored my own feelings.

I lost the connection with my body.

I lost the connection with my inner being.

I lost the love reservoir that was flowing within me whenever I offered support to others and got into the mode of pleasing others unnecessarily.

This was nothing but I was raging against my own self!

Look closely, the word 'Courage' has the rage inherently hidden within.

My mind-body connection was just snapped.

My heart and head and hand were not in sync with each other.

I was only living in my head and instructing my

hand to follow, skipping my own heart which kept whispering to me- *listen, dear, listen! stand up for your own sake but with love.*

This loss of self was unbearable and my own sense of being was questioned within me.

This is what Leon VanderPol, author of the book -A shift in being' calls the state of 'Inner Earthquake'.

What followed was all lava– anger, heat, agony, pain, despair, shame, guilt, deep annoyance and immense pain!

This time, I had to figure out what to do? How to deal with such a situation in my life?

What did I miss in this journey?

How did I get to this shape? What led me here?

Why is this happening to me?

I tried to take advice and all the respected elders told me that life happens like this for all of us, it's a phase. Have faith, time will heal 'Waqt hai– beet jayega'.

Always wondered- 'how?'

My previous approaches and patterns of behaviour were barriers in my own healing and transformation.

1. 'Ignore' – not working, others actions continued to hurt
2. 'Move on'– not working, as I felt stuck
3. 'Look at the bright side, chin up and get going'-- not working, as my body revolted

4. 'Not believing that others have a role to play in my life'-- not working, as I needed support

to recover from this stage of physical breakdown.

I found myself behaving differently---

Shutting down was never the option that I had kept for me but I was moving away from places and people who were a reminder of pain for me. I would weep, yell and feel the heat in my own body.

Most overwhelming phase for me…

Each memory of the past haunted the deepest cell in my body, sleepless nights, mental unrest and chaos.

My aches worsened. My heart broke and I was living with what I never imagined to be living with.

This was an out of syllabus situation and I had no checkpoint to live up to. (I badly needed guidance on navigating this phase of my life)

Then had to leave my job due to ill health.

Over the last 17-18 years, the compromises I made were not acknowledged in the family I sacrificed myself for– My choices? My dressing? My places of interest, even jobs– NO VALIDATION!

In my moments of despair, my 'no complaint' attitude was just thrown out of the window and all I had to talk about was 'complaints but with care' so that I didn't hurt others, while doing so.

Didn't know how to process this anger because what I could anticipate from the other person is justification and loads of dismissal and denials.

There were many suggestions and judgements,

I thought I never judged anyone but faced a lot of them.

At 40, my heart was full of regret and resentment and I acknowledge it. (*I don't know what gave me the strength to choose not to live this way for the rest of my life, which I will talk about in the next few chapters.*)

In that phase of my life, I felt the most vulnerable and edged to the corners within myself, the worst to feel within and I had no way to express this annoyance with self.

Like they say, 'try sharing' so I shared and shared and shared for days and nights with my spouse, my parents and wrote on a paper and shared as a stranger in mindfulness sessions and read and shared whatever my head and heart wanted to bring up to the people who claimed that they loved me. It helped me bring clarity to guide myself in the wanting of my heart, slowly and with love.

I realized that it was more about me and less about them. It hit hard and pained even more!

The process of mental de-cluttering was initiated because I had to transform my life and create a new living experience for me and my family.

Facing my own fears, followed by examining this duality of 'finding love' and 'living for love', I began to inquire-

- What might be 'love' looking, without an act of love?
- Is love a space within which every other emotion resides?
- How do we operate in the world with love?

- Can I fight in love?
- Can I argue in love?
- Can fear, anger and love stay together?
- How are people navigating their lives in such a situation?

My quest began and I couldn't find one fellow traveler who could understand what I was going through without offering advice or suggestions. It felt like an unknown journey where I couldn't figure out the destination.

I only needed to reconnect with myself. The love that I was seeking outside had to be sourced from within.

We don't simply change from the outside; we transform from within. Let's remember this.

Understanding Emotional Wounds and how they impact the body

The climax reached when my body refused to follow my brain. It almost went into strike mode.

I was shaken with toothache, inflammation, vaginal infections, stiffness in my spine and waking up each morning with a stiff back. I don't know why we normalize body pains in the modern way of living. One has to be aware that these pains are messages from the body–to pause, breathe, relax and sleep to let it repair itself. Also, take some necessary steps to work on the mental or emotional health.

I didn't give my body enough rest and pause that it demanded to witness pain. But, my dear reader, you start doing it for yourself.

I didn't give myself the 'Permission to feel' all the emotions. I blocked some and allowed only some as **'Staying positive and looking at the**

bright side' was the mantra I followed diligently in my life. Choose yours wisely.

This was like embracing only the daylight but not liking the night. How is that even possible?

In this way of living, we miss out on the key principle that we learnt in science classes– *'Energy can neither be created nor destroyed-it can only change form.'*

Emotions are nothing else but *'energy in motion'*. Our physical body acts like a container that carries this energy and while in motion, each emotion originates during various life situations that is either 'Expressed or Suppressed'.

(To Suppress is to stop something from being seen or known, no acknowledgement and acceptance)*

When 'expressed well' it leads to a release and

when suppressed it just is stored in the body.

Let me explain this second term further. 'Suppression' refers to the conscious and active effort to block or ignore emotions, while depression is a mental health condition characterized by persistent sadness, loss of interest, and other symptoms like fatigue and sleep disturbances. Suppression can contribute to depression by hindering the processing and expression of emotions, potentially leading to emotional bottling and stress.

The longer we take to pay attention to it, the harder it becomes in form and emerges as a disaster that leads to a total shutdown from work, people and self (like in my case).

Science has proven that the body stores pain resulting from stuck emotions and experiences accumulated over months and years. Creating new thought patterns help us feel differently. That's why affirmations work.

Here is what many other Eastern and Western healing modalities that I have used and still use to help myself release and let go of the unwanted feelings or thoughts to bring relief to the body and mind.

- Chakra healing- It is about working on the energy centers within our body. Once the centers are working well, there is harmony of feeling- thinking and doing.
- Emotional Freedom Technique (EFT) a is tapping method that helps by tapping some points on the body. It helps in releasing the stuck emotions like anxiety, worry. By bringing awareness

through our body, we change the way we think and feel.

- NLP- Neuro Linguistic Programming, only to understand how the brain works and cognitively, how do we function well. This helps in better communication skills and building interpersonal intelligence.
- Trauma Response Management – using strategies like grounding to acknowledge pains and take intentional, compassionate action.
- Mindfulness- Living in the present moment works tremendously well in establishing harmony between the mind and the body. Paying attention and being in non-judgmental awareness are my go-to practices.

- Heart to Heart conversations- open, and vulnerable sharing in the community, helps one know that I am not alone and it is the drama of life that we all get trapped in. So, the spirit of oneness gets established.

My autoimmune healing journey- my body spoke what my heart couldn't

I remember visiting a doctor, who gave me and my family a glimpse of how such diseases get triggered in the body due to persistent stress and bad lifestyle. There wasn't any genetic factor present but the presence of the dis-ease confirmed that something is not going well within the body.

The Rheumatologist looked at my medical history- correlated with my current symptoms, long enduring pains, treatments and diagnosed that I had Ankylosing Spondylitis (AS) or the Bamboo Spine Syndrome.

AS is a type of arthritis that causes inflammation in the joints and ligaments of the spine. It may also affect peripheral joints like the knees, ankles, and hips. Normally, the joints and ligaments in the spine help us move and bend. Ankylosing spondylitis has no known specific cause, though genetic factors seem to be involved. In particular, people who have a gene called HLA-B27 are at a greatly increased risk of developing ankylosing spondylitis but this may not manifest in their bodies owing to a better lifestyle and healthy thought patterns etc.

My gene test was negative but my life history showed periods of chronic stress and poor lifestyle choices. This awareness was reassuring for me because I was hopeful that if I release stress and adopt a healthy lifestyle, lose weight- I had chances of reversing the condition and be out of medication.

Two quick action steps for me were:

First, I had to learn to accept this condition and take proper medication without any blame shifting.

Second, lose weight to ease my muscles of the burden they were carrying at the physical level and I was aware of the internal weight of my unprocessed grief and sadness. Switching to plant-based diet, Yoga and meditation were my rituals, each day.

This sounds like a treatment for the physical body but until I worked on my emotional wounds, no change was possible. Accepting this fact was hard, compared with popping pills and continue living life of ignorance and disharmony.

This time I needed a sustainable shift in my life which was only possible by reconnecting with myself. What magic will help me heal completely, I didn't know then?

Like many of us, acknowledging the presence of big word- STRESS and TRAUMA, felt unacceptable…

My mind was against me and would make me believe that everything is okay but just the body is in a bad condition and has some pains with some unresolved conflicts, what else…

- How can stress be a factor of such excruciating pains that I felt emotionally and mentally?
- Why did the doctor ask me to practice forgiveness and gratitude?

The story in my head, the narratives of the past that I survived every storm in a heroic manner refused to be with this idea of forgiveness and it was a disbelief that gratitude will help in shifting my reality. That too when I am now the sufferer of the deeds and ignorance of others actions. The Victimhood kicked in.

The 'let go' of the past that I was living, wasn't an easy option. I am the one who has lived those 'bitter experiences of the past' hoping that one day it will all just be okay. People will realize how they are causing pains in the very relationship they call 'dear'.

My story, my life, my heroic journey- I couldn't believe that I have to 'let go' and 'forgive' in order to heal myself.

Yet, whenever I spoke about my pains accumulated in the past, everybody dismissed saying, "let bygones be bygones"- "past it past"- "it's over–let it go!"

The same courageous me had to now do this for my own sake.

Hard hitting reflection surfaced- What have I really lived for?

No job (I loved it so much)

No health (Severe body aches, an inflammatory condition)

No money (Only savings, no regular source)

No Joy (my sense of self was breaking)

No sense of fulfilment (I saw myself as a working woman, now what?)

No choices to make? Big question

One of the darkest incidents that happened during this time was- getting annoyed with my children. I was throwing anger and frustration on them too.

I tore a family photograph and simply isolated myself from everybody. That's just a grave reminder of the chronic state of depression; I was slipping into. Deep down, I was feeling lonely. My ego self was at work, so it was

Me vs. Everybody.

FATAL INDEED!

For years, I resisted pain and now I was causing pain to people I love. This was a vicious cycle- I got trapped.

THANK GOODNESS THAT I MADE A CHOICE TO COME BACK from this point.

This retaliation laid the foundation of my healing journey!

Pain causes more Pain

Anger causes more Anger

Resentment caused more moments of living in Resentment

I wondered if I apply the same formula of what goes around comes around-

Would love would attract more love?

It was my heart that I started paying attention to.

This strange state emerged as a storm and I had no boat to sail through. It was like standing at the shore of my presence and just waiting for this storm to take its course and settle. By that time, I could be an observer and an inquirer to go deep within the depths of my soul to seek the understanding of this process. Practicing mindfulness worked for me.

I couldn't be the previous self who lived to ignore feelings and pains, always ran from asserting myself at the cost of my own comfort, and now has to stay home and recover.

Everything had come to a standstill.

I just didn't know- How to navigate now?

It just felt that I could be one identity– Being a seeker! That felt like an inner calling which had to be explored.

No compass

No direction

No map

Earlier, I could always see the boat and knew that this job change or house change will take me to the other so embracing change never felt awkward.

Hitting this crumbling space to be no longer 'Who I have been?' was utterly uncomfortable. It was like someone robbed me of my own existence as the identities were shifting.

My own perception of myself was shifting within me. Life felt like a vast space and I was alone on this journey, not physically, but emotionally, mentally and a deeper calling was emerging- unclear, unstructured and no guidance to follow.

At that time, my biggest guides were Books- treasure of wisdom and experiences that other people have lived.

I held on to this hope-- I am seeking something; something must be seeking for me too!

Online sessions on mindfulness, trauma resilience training, healing techniques, yoga, changing food patterns, spending time in nature, talking to loved ones, journaling, gratitude practices- an array of actions on daily basis helped.

Inherently, within my being, I always held onto one belief in higher power and supreme consciousness that has plans for all of us. If it was my time to listen to this higher power then I must learn to be patient enough to let this process unfold within me.

Many of us just stick to the stories of what happened, who did that rude behaviour or disrespected us in a situation or simply rejected our presence at a family event etc, etc. It doesn't bring any shift; we must abandon these stories to break the loop of suffering.

We all hold the truth of our own existence

We create this narrative in our mind that I'm the one adjusting to everything in order to keep people together but little do we realise that we all hold the truth of our own existence into this world. The fact is that the more we don't embrace it, the more misery we create for ourselves. This story or narrative shapes our self-concept and the moment, somebody asks to drop the story, 'Nothing to hang onto' is felt within.

Like, in my case, I was adjusting, embracing the challenges of life, always running for increasing material prosperity in my home and once I achieved all of it, I didn't know- What next?

But deep within the chase, I could always sense the burden that I had started carrying, the burden of ignorance of the emotional emptiness that was creeping within.

It requires an open mind, open will and an open heart that feels to sit at the shore-PAUSE- Observe-REFLECT and allow what is wanting to unfold for me through the cracks. Asking for support is crucial for healing and even if we have one person to have a free, non-judgmental and explorative conversation, is enough. My spouse and other family members have supported me, but we need a range of social interactions and fortunately, we all have many people around us. Everybody has something to offer us.

In my case, I had this need to share the mysteries that I could feel intuitively, but looked very different from the societal narrative and explanation of a successful life. So, I feel fortunate that I have a brother, keenly interested in understanding life through astrology, drama and personal stories. He would sometimes keep encouraging me to be patient and enjoy the PAUSE in life.

I never wanted this phase but it was there. He would often say- "People don't get to rest, you are getting it, just be with it. Stop chasing or running but still move on from the past experiences to explore the new." Talking to him always felt like a sweet breeze of hope. My spouse has been supportive too but I had deeper cracks to address in our relationship as well.

When R.A was diagnosed, he would care for me and I never liked this much attention from his side. Initially, it felt uncomfortable and really unusual.

I kept asking myself- 'This is what I always wanted and now I have it- why am I not enjoying it?' This duality of thought and feeling made me realize that the repair work was needed within me, how to do it - still unclear.

You would wonder- it was just one dis-ease in the body that needed medication. But deep inside us, our consciousness emerges a whisper -- to pay attention to something sitting at the root of every illness that the body goes through.

I had read somewhere– that the body restores its state of balance and is an intelligent system with an inbuilt repair, reset mechanism. Now, in my auto-immune condition I wondered what happened to this tendency of my body. I didn't want to feel dis-empowered, therefore, I had to face the darkness within to find my light. I questioned myself-

- What did I do that didn't let my body heal?

- What emotional cleaning is needed for me?
- How to do all this work?

This led to discovering many ways, approaches and modalities that I explored to help my body restore and come out of medication. Those severe aches and stiffness have reduced now.

My mind is clear and my heart is totally taken care of.

I have restored the alignment of the 3 H- HEAD, HEART and HAND through healing and re-establishing harmony into my being.

A path of self-awareness, self-love and practicing self-compassion is what has helped and still helping me in this journey.

It was through my body that I had to redesign my life to emerge as a newer self- on a newer path to wisdom and purpose. One may say that soul searching begins here, I would say it was the meaning-making process of the entire drama that I had lived so far.

All the past incidents were data points for me and I had to be non-judgmental and practice non-attachment to those events because I was on a soul quest. As a history student, I loved exploring the past because it has a deeper connection to shaping our present lives.

It is our histories that help us trace progress and human evolution on this planet!

This journey could be undertaken with my spirit as my guide. Inner resourcing was all I could resort to.

Somewhere deeply- I was aware that it's more about me and less about anybody else because they have their own paths to navigate.

Painful moments open door for awakening

That sense of ownership of my own pains, my own body, my own emotional breakdowns, melting points due to deep stored emotion was the key to unlocking this newer sense of self that is making this book possible and is leading me to share my own story, my own truth and trauma with the world.

I hope that my story helps you explore that 'Pains and Problems' are definitely not to be sought after but these are beautiful opportunities to believe that something bigger is going to happen within me or a shift is wanting to happen in my reality.

All that you can do is to have faith and courage to embrace your pains, tend to these and just begin by coming back home i.e. within the body.

This body holds its own intelligence and wisdom. Interestingly, the body always lives in the present. It is the mind that keeps swinging to the past and future like a pendulum.

Staying with the body helps the soul sense emerge and we can seek fulfilment i.e. living a life of purpose and meaning. As human beings, we have the capacity to take ourselves to newer dimensions of love, power and purpose, to not only improve the quality of our lives but uplift others around us too.

Yet, each of us have our own journeys. The biggest lesson that my disease/illness helped me learn was– <u>'Respect everybody's journey'</u>

Don't run to fix

Don't impede the process

Don't impose your learnings

Don't interfere with their MESS!

Trust that there is a higher power looking after all of us! You may call it with whatever name and give it any form that helps you connect and feel grounded within your own self.

Chapter 3

The Silent Weight of an unfelt pain

"Awareness is the first step to healing."

– Dean Ornish

Why we suppress pain and how it manifests in our lives

In the rut of living through different roles– a teacher, a mother, a wife, a daughter, a sibling, a daughter-in-law and so on, I never realized that doing these roles to perfection was causing harm than doing any good.

We all have a finite reservoir of energy each day.

All this energy gets consumed while we perform our daily duties. The days were filled with a routine of getting up–going to work–coming back–repeating the cycle with chores like cooking, washing, dusting etc. These are essential actions of daily life.

I started with an inquiry on how and when I learnt to suppress my own emotions. Also, is it just me going through a phase or something fundamental is missing from our lives. As an educator, I didn't learn coping mechanisms and self-care routines, I wondered what's missing in our education system altogether.

- Are we talking about Life in our classrooms?

- Are we talking about Life in our homes to our children?
- What are telling them about this beautiful human life?

As a young adult, I always longed to find out about life and now here I was in a state where perhaps, I had to make a journey to explore it first hand, using my own skills and understanding of the beauty of life and how it breaks to set us free from so many limiting beliefs and values that actually, are not our own. These are stories and external narratives of how life should be. This thinking causes suffering and the mismatch in what have and what we want to have. It pushes us to operate from a space of lack not abundance.

Somewhere deep within me I felt limited in pin-pointing exactly how I was feeling in my mind and my body. This limited range of emotional expression would have caused chaos because conflicts are not always presented as good or bad. The micro- moments of pain and despair, frustration and anger, sorrow and guilt were all felt within me but I think I never acknowledged this presence because being nice, polite and always smiling had become my innate nature even in times of intense pain and grief of not knowing myself enough.

No one could gauge that I was suffering at an internal level emotionally. I had learnt to mask as my coping mechanism, perhaps. All this happens at a subconscious level of our existence. This response was ingrained so deeply that in the interest of maintaining peace, I wouldn't voice my concerns in my closest relationships.

As I reflect back now, I think I also didn't trust the relationships and the capacity of people to understand my point and wanted to avoid any sort of conflict. This expectation of no results with my own assumptions of their behavior refrained me from even trying.

As they say, keep trying until you get to the point with the other person.

But, in the deepest of my dilemmas, whenever I even made an attempt, I was the one who was left broken even more. The surge of emotions was felt and I just stopped trying. My own authentic self-expression started fading away and a lot of assumptions sat in.

The more I wanted peace, the more situations I had to manage to restore peace.

I couldn't figure out my own emotions, my own inner clarity of what I wanted from that communication and also missed out on acknowledging this fact that many of us are wired to defend and not develop, reject and not recognize. It is because their ego self would prevent them from trying to understand.

In this fast-paced life, we have conflicts all around us. The least is the home, where we don't expect but sadly, it is the most intimate relationships at home that cause more harm than any other relationship. What does your experience tell you?

In the process of living with my body pains, I would run to the doctor to get it fixed but had no way to tend to my suppressed emotions. Those pains had become deep traumas now and were well settled in my body.

The 'silent submission' never helped and it never can. It is an act of self-sabotage and no one else but we do it to ourselves.

Growing up, I never knew that there social and emotional skills that we all can learn. Self-awareness is a skill to cultivate with effort and persistence.

Another awareness that hit me was that my constant source of love was external and limited to my own children and many of my students who I felt, loved me deeply. It was always a sense of fulfilment to be with them. Professional and personal lives stood in contrast to each other at some point in my life and I felt like being split, but I was the same person.

I grew curious to know what's working professionally but not working personally.

Why did I feel torn inside? No idea.

Emotional Literacy: Naming and Processing Deep Emotions

"Hurt feelings don't vanish on their own. They don't heal themselves. If we don't express our emotions, they pile up like a debt that will eventually come due"- March Brackett, author of Permission to Feel

During my work as educator, as part of the Character Culture Team, I came across this lovely framework and approach that I needed more than anybody, I felt. It was during our online classes that we would help our learners navigate social and emotional skills to help them process their emotions and learn to channelize their energy in a more constructive manner.

Prior to this framework, I never knew that such literacy also exists in this world. That we can give ourselves Permission to FEEL, how interesting and relevant this work is for all of us.

It sparked a reflection in me- Have I not given myself the permission to Feel my own emotions?

One of the most phenomenal works that I came across is this book by Dr. Marc Brackett, called – 'Permission to Feel'. It helped me question myself if I have blocked or not allowed myself to feel a full range of emotions that must have emerged within me, until that point in my life.

- If yes- How did it impact me and my relationships?
- If No- How did it impact me and my relationships?

This knowledge helped me at an individual level to learn and develop my emotional vocabulary, and that I need to be an 'emotional scientist' and not an 'emotion judge'. Let me experience this range of emotions through my body and my mind.

It was still heavy to live with the heaviest emotions that were filled in my most valuable milestones of life as I stayed more with unpleasantness than pleasantness.

It allowed me to discover that I had to do something within to process the tough emotions tied to my memories of the past. The wounds of the past inexpressiveness were still present in the form of mental pain and emotional pain.

<u>Here is the tool from this book, that you might like to use:</u>

RULER – acronym to remember the 5 skills of emotional intelligence:

- Start with **R**ecognizing emotions in oneself and others
- Try **U**nderstanding the causes and consequences of these emotions
- Pick appropriate words for **L**abelling emotions
- Choose **E**xpressing emotions in accordance with cultural norms and social context
- Begin **R**egulating emotions with helpful strategies

These vital skills can be used to help people of all ages. It is necessary to optimize our emotions wisely, opening opportunities for us to succeed in school, at work, and in life. These skills are both personal and social, such that a network emerges with positive changes reinforced.

Identifying, naming and processing emotions is one of the most revolutionary works that I have come across. It has the power to transform expression and help us process and channelize tough emotions and feelings like guilt, sadness, annoyance and resentment with greater understanding without becoming overwhelmed. This work brought phenomenal emotional awareness to me.

The inner breaking was unfortunate, unsolicited and unwanted. It still was happening as I navigated my life while managing R.A, medicines and changing my diet pattern, sleep pattern etc.

My next quest was to find out and learn–

How to process the sadness and grief that has filled my dearest of relationships?

I was split in my heart and my head. Didn't

understand who to listen to. The thought level change was still not figured out.

How unprocessed grief and trauma shapes our relationships

We like it or not, experiencing some form of grief is an integral part of human life. It might not be wanted but with love there is pain so with joy, there is some grief in life.

After all, Life is an emotional rollercoaster ride!

Think of the fun when you swing up and then go down to swing back up! enjoyable and exciting indeed. It brings thrill to the entire experience!

When we go down, we know it's not permanent and wait for the swing to go up again, in its own time and as per its speed…what we do once we are on the ride…just surrender with faith- in the swing, on the operator and notice that there are others also going through the same ride. (Use your discretion and do your safety checks though)

Let's apply this same analogy to this passage of life, which is a huge and long rollercoaster, it has ups and downs and all we can do and must do is to surrender to its flow. There is an operator and, it's reassuring to know that I am not the only one going through the down phase of life.

I am not saying that we expect bad for us or anybody else but, just sit with this acceptance that there will be moments of ecstasy, love, joy which may be replaced by some moments of sadness, pain and frustration.

Nothing remains the same forever!

Look at nature, how beautifully the cyclic

patterns continue to form day and night. It is important to process the reasons as long-standing grief becomes a trauma, because we haven't been able to address it and have rather learnt to shun it.

I have learnt that processing Grief leads to Growth which helps one live with Grace. Think about it and journal if you may like to.

Another way to approach---One of the most amazing analogies we use in mindfulness is to check what's in my cup.

Check your cup of life- Is your cup filled with sorrow, heartache or anguish?

Ask your yourself- What am I giving to my loved ones, if not this?

It might be in the form of losing temper often at work, in home; not understanding perspectives of your spouse or your parents; being too pushy with your own children etc.

Social withdrawal, difficulty in concentrating, irregular sleep patterns, staying anxious - are all such behaviors that are manifestations of unprocessed grief within an individual.

It simply breaks your own relationship with yourself. It can be understood as one's inability to accept loss and resolve sadness. Operating through this state since childhood, results in emotional numbness, abandonment of self and also isolation, leading to more sorrow and disintegration.

Case Study 1

Meera's Story – When Love Collides with Unhealed Pain

Meera, a 42-year-old successful marketing executive and mother of two, always prided herself on being strong, independent, and reliable. On the surface, her life looked ideal — a stable marriage, two bright children, and a beautiful home in a metro city. But behind the carefully curated life was a woman silently battling an invisible storm.

Meera lost her mother suddenly when she was just 14. The shock of the loss was too heavy for her teenage self to process, and in a family that didn't talk about emotions openly, she quickly learned to suppress her grief. She was told to "be strong," "focus on studies," and "not make things harder for her father." Without realizing it, Meera locked her grief away in a dark corner of her being — hidden but very much alive.

Years later, that unprocessed grief began to show up in her relationships, especially with her husband, Arjun. While he longed for emotional intimacy and open conversations, Meera often shut down during conflict. She didn't know how to express sadness or ask for support. Any time he brought up an issue, she felt instantly blamed — as if she was failing again to protect the people she loved. Her nervous system had learned to associate emotional confrontation with threat, and her default coping mechanism was to emotionally withdraw or become overly controlling.

She also struggled deeply with her children's big emotions. Her daughter's tears would trigger an unexplained wave of helplessness and irritation in her. She later realized that her discomfort came from seeing her own ungrieved inner child reflected in her daughter's vulnerability — something she had been conditioned to ignore for decades.

It wasn't until Meera developed an autoimmune condition in her late thirties that she began to examine her inner life. Through therapy, mindfulness practices, and inner child healing work, she uncovered how her body had carried the weight of unspoken grief and how that unresolved trauma had subtly shaped her sense of safety in relationships.

She slowly began the process of grieving — not just the loss of her mother, but also the loss of emotional safety, the loss of a childhood where feelings were allowed to exist. As she released her pain through tears, journaling, and somatic healing, she noticed subtle yet powerful changes. She became more present with her children, learned to sit with discomfort instead of fixing it, and began to share her true emotions with her husband — not as a sign of weakness, but as an invitation for deeper connection.

Meera's story illustrates a profound truth: when grief goes unprocessed, it doesn't disappear — it embeds itself in our emotional responses, our relationships, and even our physical health. Healing is not about forgetting or moving on; it's about finally giving ourselves the permission to feel what we were once too scared or too young to feel. When we do that, we don't just heal ourselves — we heal generations of unspoken pain. Isn't it powerful?

Case Study 2

Rohan's Story – The Silent Weight Men Carry

Rohan, a 45-year-old finance professional living in Mumbai, had always seen himself as the provider, the pillar, the problem-solver. Raised in a traditional household, emotions were often seen as distractions. Crying was for the weak, and vulnerability was something to be managed — not expressed.

When Rohan was 17, he failed in class XI final exam so he had to repeat his class. There is a background to this situation. He had changed his school and didn't like his new school because of the environment, also the long distance to the school. The family had relocated because of his elder brother's business and the parents' entire attention was to support the elder brother, who is 5 years elder to Rohan. His mother was a teacher and father in a govt service. Rohan didn't like travelling to school each day for almost 2 hours on one side and had to wait long for local trains in the afternoon. The frequency of trains was irregular, so the long wait at railway station was a routine for him. He would reach home by evening, after attending his school from 7:30am to 1:30pm. He was unhappy, annoyed and anxious. As a science student, he had enormous syllabus and had to study well to excel. His aspiration was to pursue MBBS.

But his failure in XI made him a reason for mockery in his extended family. The mother understood him but couldn't help him resolve the shame and stress that he was slipping into and also, guide him towards his own aspiration.

He was told to "be strong and try again". So,

he put on a brave face, buried his pain, and focused on building a successful life. He could barely pass in XII and had not prepared for MBBS, another internal collapse. He took admission to a bachelor's course and prepared for Armed forces exams. He cleared the written but never passed the interview process.

Comparisons were drawn with the elder brother, who had set up his business and was married with a child. He felt the pressure to be successful like his brother. He didn't get his space to be but was looked down as a failure or a confused man.

At 25, Rohan was still a struggler. He had tried odd jobs but couldn't crack a stable career for himself. At 27, He finally landed into a Govt job but not of his own choice. This helped restore his image in the family and he was proud of himself but was filled with agony, pain and by this time, he had learnt to suppress his own emotions while navigating failure- at school, in college and in interviews; facing comparisons and emotional unavailability of his own parents.

Years passed, but something inside him remained frozen. While Rohan loved his wife and children deeply, he struggled to emotionally connect. He was dependable, yes — but emotionally unavailable. Anubha, his wife, often described him as "present but not fully there." He didn't know how to express his inner world, and every time she tried to initiate deeper conversations, he would shut down, change the subject, or grow defensive.

His body, however, didn't stay silent. In his early forties, Rohan began experiencing chronic fatigue, intense headaches, and digestive issues. The doctors found no underlying disease. His emotional armor was beginning to crack.

A chance encounter with a colleague at work, who had just returned from a men's emotional wellness retreat, sparked something in Rohan. For the first time, he heard another man openly talk about grief, shame, and the inner emptiness that success couldn't fill. That conversation led him to therapy — and ultimately, to himself.

In the safe space of therapy, Rohan unpacked the grief that he never allowed himself to feel — the pain of losing his dreams, the pressure of becoming "the man" before he was ready, the loneliness of carrying it all alone. He realized how the unprocessed trauma had made him emotionally rigid, affecting not just his marriage but also his relationship with his teenage children, who were pressured to fulfil his dreams. They had begun to show signs of shutting down in similar ways.

The healing process wasn't instant, but it was real. Rohan began practicing breathwork and journaling. He started having slow, awkward but honest conversations with Anubha. He even took his son on a weekend retreat and shared childhood stories he had never spoken aloud. For the first time in years, he cried — and felt lighter.

Rohan's story is a reminder that unprocessed grief or sadness doesn't discriminate by gender. In cultures where men are conditioned to suppress emotions, trauma often shows up not in tears, but in distance, disconnection, and dis-ease. But healing begins the moment we stop running and start feeling. Vulnerability is not the opposite of strength — it foundational to building it with authenticity and resilience.

PART 2

"Kintsugi is built on the idea that in embracing flaws and imperfections, you can create an even stronger, more beautiful piece of art."

— Beth Kempton, *Wabi Sabi: Japanese Wisdom for a Perfectly Imperfect Life*

The healing journey:

Learning to love your brokenness

Chapter 4

Love as a catalyst for healing

"Your task is not to seek for love, but merely to seek and find all the barriers within yourself that you have built against it." — Rumi

The Essence of Love

Love is the purest of all emotions — an invisible force that every living being seeks. It has no fixed form, shape, or colour. And yet, it is the thread that binds the universe together.

Ironically, though it is *everywhere*, it is also *what*

we seem to miss the most.

This is the paradox of being human.

Love is what unifies the planet — connecting creatures, seasons, elements, and souls. In its presence, life thrives. In its absence, we wither.

Nature's Language of Love

In my observations, I have often seen how love is expressed effortlessly in nature:

- The butterfly loves the flower.
- The honeybee dances in devotion to the bloom.
- The flower — a graceful giver — blooms to welcome them during spring.

Isn't this love?

A dance of **giving and receiving**?

Another beautiful analogy is of the tree and the

earth:

A small seedling cracks open the soil to emerge. The earth surrenders.

The sapling grows, becoming a plant and then a tree — standing tall through seasons, offering shelter to birds and harmony to the land.

We humans *live* because of these plants.

Love, like nature, is a force that flows — self-sustaining, ungoverned, and boundless.

To box it, name it, or define it is to *limit* its sacred essence.

The Mind Tries, The Heart Knows

Love is not something the mind can fully understand. It is something the heart **feels**, something the soul **remembers**, and something the body **expresses**.

Love is a fleeting feeling.

Love is tenderness.

Love is an innocent smile.

Love is the gentle touch of an infant.

Love is light — and the light of love is pure.

Reflections to Ponder

- What comes to your mind when you think of love?
- Who do you believe can bring love into your life?
- Are you on an endless quest of "finding love"?
- What does *love* truly mean to you?

When Love Becomes a Cage

Throughout my journey, I've had people who

loved me — deeply and purely.

And yet, in that love, they sometimes tried to **shield, protect, or even isolate** me.

A mother's love, for instance, is considered unconditional. But sometimes, even in that love, the child can feel **restricted**.

In trying to protect, the mother may unknowingly build walls.

And then both begin to question: *Is this really love?*

We often say the problem lies in a the "generation gap."

But is it the gap between generations, or the gap between our hearts?

The Misunderstandings of Love

We often:

- Judge love
- Compartmentalize it
- Compare it
- Place expectations upon it

But love cannot be put in a box.

Love cannot be compared or measured.

Reflect and ask yourself:

1. How do I perceive love in my life?
2. Who have I made responsible for loving me?
3. What forms of love have I experienced through various relationships?

The Love We're Born Into

- We are born through an act of love.
- We are carried in the womb with love.
- We bring love and joy to our families.

- We are loved — *in different ways* — all our lives

But are we truly *feeling* it?

Or

Are we still seeking it outside us?

Love is Freedom, Not Possession

Ask a teenager what love means, and you might hear:

Freedom. Passion. Equality. Connection.

But somewhere in the real world, the narrative of love has shaped us differently, so

- Love becomes control
- Love becomes sacrifice
- Love becomes obligation
- Love becomes fear

Are we allowed to discriminate in the name of love?
Can we bind others for love of country, family, or belief?

Is it still love when it becomes about rules, roles, and responsibilities?

The Inner Realization: Love Begins Within

One of my longest explorations in this journey was:

- Where do I find love for myself?
- Am I expecting someone else to bring it into my life?
- How can someone else give me something they don't even have for themselves?

Let's explore the distorted version around us

- Is love **lust**?
- Is love **obsession**?
- Is love **control**?
- Is love **possession**?
- Is love **a condition** or a **restriction**?

Or…

Is love a gentle breeze that brings us together,

Felt in the whisper of leaves,

The song of a morning bird,

Or the stillness of the night.

Releasing the Barriers to Love

Take a moment to reflect:

- When did you build barriers to love within yourself?

- What beliefs and expectations are shaping your experience of love?

We often chase love, feel empty in our relationships,
And become our own obstacles to love.

Let this chapter be an invitation to **release** every notion, belief, or judgement of what love *should* look like for you.

Love is **not** one-size-fits-all.

We are each unique. Our expressions of love must be too.

Self-Love: The Heart of Healing

Let love take over your healing journey. Let it **guide** you, **nurture** you, and **hold** your broken pieces gently.

"Self-love is not selfish. It is sacred."

Think of your brokenness as fertile soil. The seeds of love have always been there.

You simply forgot to water them. Start taking care of yourself in love and surrender to the flow.

Distinguishing Love That Heals from Love That Hurts

We must learn to differentiate between:

- Love that **heals**
- And love that **wounds**

Popular culture, movies often glorify *possessive*, *dramatic*, *codependent* love.

But true love can't be forced or controlled.

It's not "I choose for you because I love you." That's **possession**.

It's not "You must behave this way." That's

imposition.

Love as a Pathway to Transformation

In the context of this book, love is not just a theme.

It is a path, it's the process and it's a life-long journey.

A gentle force leading us toward **healing**, **transformation**, and **wholeness**.

I leave it to you to choose your path:

- Will you walk it with **love**, or with **fear**?

Love and Fear can't stay together, so be aware of your style of operating in the world.

Cultivate Love & Self-Compassion

"You can't pour from an empty cup."

Mindfulness practices have taught me to check — *What's in my cup?*

Is it shame, guilt, resentment?

→ *Empty it with care.*

Is it peace, joy, and ease?

→ *Let it overflow.*

Be mindful of what you're pouring into your relationships.

Be open to refilling your own cup first- with love and discard what doesn't belong to you.

Forgive yourself for not knowing enough about your own self.

Forgive, if for years, you deprived yourself of the love that only you can give to yourself as a gift.

Release the burden. Release the past actions and start afresh.

Final Reflection

We all long for love.

But love has always been within us.

Let's stop chasing love as something "outside of us."

Instead, let's choose to **become** love

In our presence, in our words, in our being.

Let love be the language we speak — to ourselves, to others, to life.

A story

"The Whispering Tree"

Once upon a time in a quiet village wrapped in hills and winds, there lived a woman named Meera. Known for her gentle smile and quiet strength, she carried a weariness in her eyes that no one really noticed. On the outside, Meera's life looked perfect—a family, a home, a routine. But inside, she felt hollow. Not broken. Just... missing.

Every morning, she walked past the old banyan tree at the edge of the village. Some said it whispered to those who listened. Meera never stopped—until one morning, when something inside her tugged her to sit beneath it.

As she leaned against its ancient roots, a soft breeze rustled the leaves above her. And in that moment, she heard a whisper—not through her ears, but through her heart.

"Love is not what you lost. Love is who you are."

Startled, she looked around. No one was there.

Just the wind and the tree with her.

The words stayed.

In the days that followed, she kept returning to

the tree. She brought her journal, her tears, her silence. And each time, the tree seemed to listen. She wrote stories she never told, questions she never dared to ask, and slowly—like the first bloom of spring—she began to feel a warmth return. Not from someone else. But from within.

One day, a child from the village asked her, "Why do you sit with this tree so often?"

She smiled and said, "Because it reminds me that love doesn't always come from others. Sometimes, it waits patiently inside you, like a seed. You just need to sit still long enough to hear it whisper."

Years later, the village came to know that the banyan was no ordinary tree—it became known as "Meera's Tree," a place where people came to rest, cry, write, or simply breathe.

They say the tree still whispers.

But only to those who are ready to listen to the love they carry within.

Chapter 5

Rewriting Your Story

"What brings us to tears will lead us to grace. Our pain is never wasted." – Bob Goff

Our Beliefs Shape How We Show Up in the World

The environment we live in—the parents we have, the school, peers, relatives—all relationships we are born into determine our core beliefs as we move from childhood to adulthood.

Out of all the interactions and exchanges we have during family gatherings; the biggest determinant of a child's belief system comes from home.

Parents, grandparents, siblings—these relationships, in my experience, hold the strongest influence in shaping who we become as adults.

The magic is that, subconsciously, we operate from a similar belief system, coupled with some of our own beliefs, in all relationships we live.

The best example I can recall from my own life experience is one from my mother: **"Be good, no matter what."**

Hold on to your inner goodness. Maintain peace in the family. Women have many duties to fulfil, and adjustments must be made in the interest of the family.

Many such beliefs and values were unconsciously *imported* when I entered into relationships post-marriage.

At this point, I want to be clear—I am not judging my mother, her belief systems, or the values I've just mentioned. The effort is look through consciously to examine where is the gap.

There is no good or bad here. No right or wrong. It simply exists as it is.

Let me take you through the impact these beliefs had on my life.

(Subconsciously, I had made these beliefs mine, because we learn through imitation and follow patterns of our elders—something we know from various child development theories.)

"Be good, no matter what" became a core belief. It was fundamental to how I showed up earlier in life, and in a different way, still influences how I show up in the world now.

I can best explain this as a before-and-after picture, pre-and-post my healing and transformation journey.

In the previous version of me:

1. I hesitated to express myself—my feelings, my emotions, especially annoyance or anger.

2. Even if I thought about expressing them, I held back and began judging myself: *"It wouldn't be good."*

3. I believed I couldn't be angry in my own relationships because it would harm the

peace in the family. I thought I must adjust and wait for times to change—even if I was in pain.

4. This belief interfered with my personal well-being. I had unknowingly sent out messages to people that, even if they harmed me, I would not react. I refrained from drawing boundaries, and this encouraged others to continue harmful behavior.

5. I did not allow myself to fully feel or process stuck emotions—often because of lived experiences that shaped this response.

Today, I still carry the same belief—but with love, awareness and gentleness.

The meaning it holds for me now is different:

1. I express myself in an authentic manner, as much as I can.

2. Even if I express anger or pain, I no longer judge myself. I know I'm still holding goodness within me.

3. It is okay to feel anger, resentment, frustration. I now know how to process and express these emotions in a healthy way.

4. With self-compassion and kindness, I've learned to draw healthy boundaries in my most intimate relationships—with gentleness and love, even when overwhelmed.

5. I've given myself *permission to feel*—every emotion, every part of my lived experience. I now embrace those parts without doubt or fear or judgement.

The belief is the same, but with an increased sense of self-awareness and healing, the *quality* of my experiences has shifted.

I'm happy to share that this shift has helped me move beyond my own limits, and toward a deeper truth:

"Be good—first to yourself."

"Be good—with awareness and boundaries."

The process of finding meaning, moving away from inherited belief systems, and letting go of unhealthy ones has helped me practice a different reality—within the same relationships that once caused pain.

I felt closer to myself.

Reassured.
Full of love.

And I began to see my own family as a source

of growth—no blame. No drama. Because drama creates more drama.

I love and respect my mother. I haven't negated her role in my life. She is my biggest support system and will always be.

I look at her life with empathy and openness. She might have picked up those values from her own mother. She lived them, found them soothing, and did her best in the context and circumstances of her time.

After all, external context also plays a big role in shaping our inner world.

What I'm highlighting here is an invitation to go within.

To welcome the change—because that has the power to transform your life.

"We experience the world as we are."

It took me years to deconstruct this truth. But every effort was worth it.

As I shifted my approach toward inner beliefs, I began to experience something new in my life.

The quality of my relationship—with myself and with others—has improved gradually.

Therefore, the call is to be with yourself first. Only then will others rise to meet your energy of *being*.

The Shift from Victimhood to Empowerment

When I hit the lowest phase of my life—emotionally, physically, and mentally—after COVID, I had to ask myself:

- Am I ready to be a victim for life?
- Have I become one already?

- Who is a victim?

In simple words, as I processed it in my heart, a victim is someone who suffers. Someone who has been wronged. Someone who feels cheated, abandoned, unsupported—where circumstances seem stacked against.

It's a person who receives others' actions passively, and feels helpless, fearful, unable to act or escape.

This mental state shifts your perception. Everyone starts looking like an "abuser" or a "wrong-doer." Every situation feels unfair. The cycle of resentment takes over—and wreaks havoc on your inner world.

The self-concept gets diluted in this state. It pollutes situations, relationships, and thoughts—leading to toxic patterns.

Living in this disempowered state is *miserable.*

The sooner we recognize it, the sooner we can walk the path of empowerment.

For me, the shift began when I acknowledged and accepted the truth of my reality:

I had slipped into that state of misery. And then, I made a conscious choice.

- A choice to no longer operate from that place.
- A choice to feel differently.
- A choice to think differently.
- A choice to see differently.
- A choice to live and love differently.

This choice awakened *ownership* in me. If I don't take ownership of my own life, who will?

So, I told myself:

Whatever happened to me, with me, through
or by anyone in this world—
I accept it.
I acknowledge it.
And now, I choose to move forward—with
strength and love, grounded in my body.

Let me learn to be my own savior. Let me explore what life has been waiting to show me.

They say the universe has a plan for each of us. So, let me walk my path, and seek what is seeking me.

That inner shift redirected my energy—towards empowerment and a new reality.

The Mantra:

Embrace {life as it is}
Engage {with curiosity and presence}

Empower {yourself to walk your path through continuous learning}

"Our thoughts create our reality."

Is this true?

How?

Empowerment is only possible when we're ready to embrace our own *flaws and shadows.* Only then, our inherent thought and behavior patterns reveal themselves. Only then, we can replace those unhealthy ones with new ones.

With curiosity and love in my heart, I began to rewrite my own story.

Values like trust, courage, resilience, and gratitude—these were always within me. But now, I began to *live* them differently. With care. With surrender. With alignment to a higher consciousness.

This time, I trusted the process—without trying to control the outcome.

This time, I embraced courage gently—no more rage at the world or at myself.

This time, I was resilient—knowing that life was shaping me through every lesson that I need to learn from my own challenges and circumstances.

And I did it all with gratitude. Not just for the good that happened to me—but even for the worst events and experiences of my life.

I became thankful not just for those who stood by me, but also for those who didn't. I practiced gratitude—for the pain, my body, my parents, my partner, my children, my extended family, my colleagues...

To all those who showed up—through action or silence—I say: Thank you.

- It was tough, but I stayed hopeful.
- It pained me, but I chose the path of discovery.
- It pushed me deep into my own shadows—into questioning my beliefs, my perceptions, really uncomfortable.

For the first time, I walked an unknown path—with love, authenticity, and gentleness in my heart.

No judgement. No self-loathing. No blame.

I feel grateful to myself for choosing this path. Because it opened doors that I didn't know existed.

It helped me find purpose.

And it led me here—to write this book and share my story with passion and purpose.

If you're sitting in a place like I once did—seeking healing and transformation—know this:

It all begins with *Self*.

If you shift your thoughts and energy, it creates ripples of change inside-out.

A personal exercise: Reflect and write--In which area of your life do you want to write a *new story*? (relationships, career, health, spirituality, finances, education etc)

This is how I would describe my journey in - Being Alice in Wonderland

Alice once walked in a world so wide,
Where dreams were real and fears could hide.
But down she fell, not by design—

Into a world between heart and mind.

She met the Mad Hatter, sipping his tea,
Who said, "The only way out is to first see.
You've been chasing clocks and losing time,
But healing begins when you call it *mine.*"

The Queen of Hearts yelled, "Off with her
head!"
But Alice just smiled and breathed-in instead.
"No more shrinking to fit your crown,
I've found my voice—I won't back down."

The Cheshire Cat grinned from up in a tree,
"You're not lost, love—you're just learning to
be.
Let the madness swirl, let the chaos spin,
The wonderland lies deep within."

She met her fears and sat them to tea,
Said, "Thank you for trying to protect me.
But now I walk with courage and grace—

I've come home to my sacred space."

So, Alice didn't climb back out the hole,
She stayed and stitched back her soul.
Not with perfection, not with a plan—
But with self-love and faith hand in hand.

Now Wonderland's not some place to flee—
It's a part of her truth, wild and free.
She's not who she was, but more than
before—
A woman who broke and bloomed from the
core.

Chapter 6

Emotional Resilience – The Power of Bouncing Back

Krishna tells Arjuna in the Bhagwat Gita:

"For the one who has conquered the mind, the mind is the best friend. For one who has failed to do so, the mind is the greatest enemy."

Your mind will either be your weapon or your weakness. (*The choice is yours — let us train it.*)

Exploring Emotional Resilience

In the previous chapter, I described how learning to be resilient became a key value for me. I think I've always been resilient. I don't give up on people or relationships so easily. I keep trying — with shape-shifting persistence — to explore a common good for everyone involved.

On a personal level, resilience helped me stay strong and keep going, without malice in my heart. But when my body almost gave up — struggling with physical immobility and frequent bouts of severe mental and emotional pain — I had to unlearn some of my deeply ingrained patterns of thought and behaviour. But my mind was still not with me.

I had done some work with my thoughts, as I mentioned earlier, but it was my emotions that

I had no clue how to manage. The big questions were:

- How do I regulate my emotions — without suppressing them?
- How do I express what I feel clearly, without being overwhelmed?
- What do I do with the tough feelings?
- How do I stay authentic and kind to others around me?

One of the dilemmas- Now that I have decided to rewrite my story…

  - Who are the characters in this story?
  - Which new characters have to come in?
  - Which of the old ones must be released?

  - What should I give importance to in this part of my story?

These questions would cross my mind constantly. I was puzzled to the core.

1. Can I rewrite my story with the same characters?
2. If yes — am I the hero this time?
3. If no — do I even have a choice?
4. Should I change the setting entirely? (move to a new place an find new job)

These ponderings led me to discover strength and clarity within myself. I always thought I knew who I was — but I realized, not enough. There was so much more about me waiting to be explored.

One of the most profound ways we learn about ourselves is through others. It is this *relationality*

— the connections we share — that becomes a mirror. The relationships we enter into, the people we attract into our lives, all have a significant role to play in our development and growth.

After all, every story needs characters — and it is the characters that keep it going.

Just like in movies, the hero needs an antagonist to rise. Supporting characters help in bringing twist to the story. There are battles to fight. Treasures to find. A cause to stand up for. Etcetera, etcetera.

What do you think?

The Unknown in Relationships

In our human lives, we're governed by situations that are often unknown to us. Similarly, entering relationships is like stepping into a blend of the known and the unknown — constantly evolving. Even a lifetime of exploration isn't enough to discover everything about ourselves or others.

At this point, I want to talk about *emotional resilience.*

- Do these two words sound heavy together?
- Don't they feel like jargon?

And yet, they hold the key to deep personal development and transformation.

Understanding "Emotion"

Before we explore "resilience," let's understand one of my favorite words — *emotion.*

We all experience emotions. There's a vast range of them. We connect with others through our emotions — deeply rooted ones — often at a subconscious level, whether we're aware or not.

So, in my journey, I asked: How do I become emotionally resilient?

Earlier in life, whenever I tried to express my pain, I was left with more pain. Whenever I got angry — honestly and vulnerably — in relationships at home or at work, people believed something was *wrong* with me. That led to a vicious cycle of arguments. Everyone held onto their own "truths," with no resolution in sight.

It became a never-ending tug of war with trying to prove-

- Who is right?
- Who suffered more?
- Who is adjusting more?

Each question only deepened frustration and resentment — leading to unrest within me. I needed a solution not more problems or arguments.

When I reflected, I would often wonder in silence:

- Did I miss the point? (*Self-doubt*)
- Maybe the other person just doesn't have the capacity to understand? (*Judgement*)
- Maybe I need to try harder next time, in a different way? (*Still missing the point…*)

I think many of us go through a similar phase in our relationships — where we either give up or give into or resist. None of this actually helps.

Are you facing a similar situation in your life

right now?

- Have you been through such a phase?
- How did you navigate it with kindness and love in your heart?

Personal insights on overcoming setbacks with mindfulness.

"We are not our best intention — we are what we do."
— Amy Dickinson

This journey helped me discover a fundamental truth: **Emotions are energy.**

Energy cannot be created or destroyed. It only changes form.

I used to wonder about this phrase- *"What goes around comes around."*

It made sense to me when I realized:
-If I'm throwing out anger, I'll get more of it.

-If I'm living in resentment, I'll receive more of that too.

So, what if I turn it around?

What if I start showing up differently in the world? (my eureka moment!)

That small curiosity sparked new patterns of thinking. My thoughts changed, and with that, my actions, daily habits changed.

Here's a powerful visual that helped me understand the relationship between thoughts, feelings, and behavior — and ultimately, who we become.

I have it always ready on the display board near my desk.

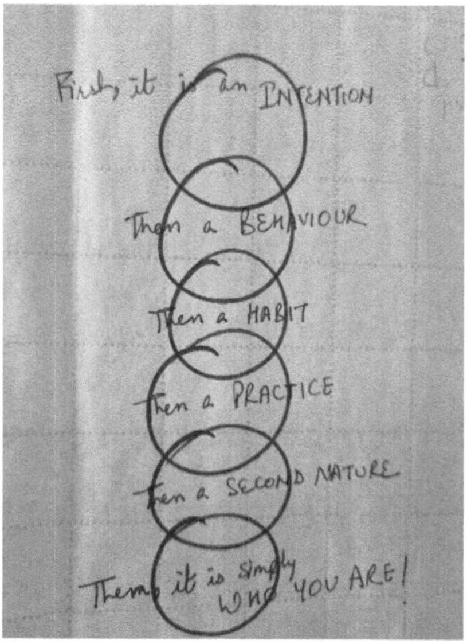

This image stays with me and gives me hope: **When I change, things around me will change too.**

I wasn't ready to sit in passive victimhood anymore. I didn't want life to "happen to me."

I chose to become a *seeker* of a new reality. I believed that if the universe has created each of us as powerful, whole, and loving, then

why are we choosing to feel powerless, broken, and unloved?

What do you think of emotional resilience?

Taking Ownership

Reconnecting with my core was a deep calling. Taking full responsibility meant practicing it in every moment — through pain, sorrow, and joy — without guilt, remorse, or shame.

This task was much harder than I imagined. **Can you relate to this experience?**

My emotional energy was waiting to be transformed.

Fortunately, I was working as a Master Trainer for the course -Social and Emotional Learning with UNESCO MGIEP (2022–23, 2023–24). That period helped me cultivate greater compassion and empathy — especially towards myself.

The more I heard people feeling hurt, judged, or ignored, the more I realized I wasn't alone. There are many others carrying pain, shame, guilt, loneliness, and isolation in their heart.

I learned to cultivate love and practice compassion even during pain and found healthier ways to express my feelings.

Collective Healing

Sometimes, healing begins when we realize we are not alone. But during moments of suffering, the pain feels intense and heavy. We shut down. We wait for someone to understand — but don't say a word.

This behaviour pushes us into **hopelessness** and **numbness**. I was surrounded by people

— yet deeply alone inside.

That kind of emotional state can be **fatal.**

It leads to:

- A distorted view of self and others
- Passive aggression
- Constant conflict — within and outside
- Emotional detachment and burnout

I had entered a "warrior mode" that was always switched on. Emotional detachment and disconnect with others resulted in detachment and disconnection with self.

What mode are you practicing each day?

Let's remember that re-establishing connection with self and others is vital for healing. (Ironic, isn't it — in this hyperconnected age of social media?)

Reflective Activity:

Spend some quiet time with yourself and notice how are you operating in your world. Write how you feel, think or wonder within you, and reflect on:

- What connections/ disconnections are you living each day?
- What are your actions reflecting about your intentions and thoughts?
- Is there a mismatch between your thoughts, intentions and your actions?

Mindful Practices: Overcoming Setbacks

Emotional resilience as a theory can be defined as an individual's ability to remain calm, positive, and emotionally capable during difficult situations. Be aware that there will always be bumps on the road, the idea is to develop skills that make the journey beautiful.

It involves:

1. Emotional flexibility
2. The ability to bounce back from adversity
3. Effective coping strategies

Building blocks of Emotional resilience are

- Social support
- Emotional regulation
- Self-awareness

Here's a helpful A–Z of mindful choices:

Adapting instead of Annoyance

Bouncing back instead of bottling up

Coping strategies instead of criticism/complaints

Developing connection over disconnection

Empathizing instead of emptiness

Flexibility instead of fear/ fussing around

Gratitude instead of grumpiness

Humility instead of hope over hostility

Introspection instead of impulsiveness

Joy instead of judgement/jealousy

Kindness instead of cruelty

Love instead of lamenting

Mindfulness instead of mindlessness

Novelty instead of normalcy

Openness instead of opinions

Process instead of performance

Quality conversation instead of quarrels

Respect instead of remorse/ resistance

Sustaining instead of succumbing

Truth instead of triumph

Understanding instead of undermining

Volition instead of volatility

Wonder instead of worry

Xercise instead of exclusion

Yin–Yang instead of yo-yo-ing

Zeal instead of zoning out

Each pair represents a conscious *choice.* Healing begins with choice — without it, the journey to change and transformation is just a longing but not a lived reality.

My motto-*"I become what I choose to be."*

I want you to believe in the power of your own choices. Life throws everything at us- pain and pleasure, good and bad, ugly and beautiful experiences. It is the meaning that we attach to it. The key is to be open and willing to choose one but not to shun the other, let it be there, don't engage if that helps your healing.

Also, remember that choices have consequences- healthy or unhealthy, that depends again on your personal goals, interest and aspirations. You alone have the ability to shape your life — through your relationships with self and work, and your moments with your loved ones.

Let's remind ourselves to be wiser, calmer, and softer from this moment onwards and choose practices that support our healing and wellbeing, such as…

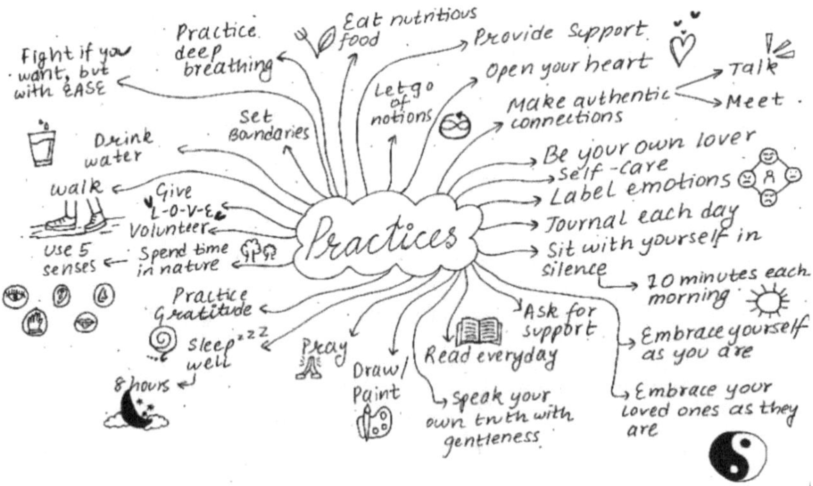

Be aware --Not making any choice is a choice too!

My life is a reflection of the values I hold dear and the actions I took willingly or unwillingly. It's a total package and we need to be open to receiving with grace and surrender.

Each mistake, failure, hurt and challenge are part of a whole — a journey into wholeness.

Nature has created yin and yang, black and white, light and dark, creation and destruction, life and death — happening together side by side in some divine rhythm.

Connect more to the rhythm and be one with it, with will, practice and intentional action.

Lessons to learn

I wanted to control the outcome and be "right." That limited my ability to accept people and situations as they *were* — not as I *wanted* them to be.

I thought I could do great things with courage — but forgot to be gentle with myself.

I missed surrendering with faith in the divine flow and timing.

Coming back home to my body helped me tune into a deeper wisdom as I intentionally created movement from an ego-centric life to a soul-centric one.

Reflect and write

Consider the choices you want to make at this stage of your life? Write them in a journal and choose your daily actions.

PART 3

"Trauma happens in relationships, so it can only be healed in relationships. Art cannot provide healing and therapeutic relationship is a separate journey."

— Alexis Mauritius

Finding Wholeness: Becoming more you

Chapter 7

The Courage to Feel Everything

"Nobody changes until you change your energy."

— Dr. Joe Dispenza

I had always perceived **"courage"** as a trait that helps in dealing with the outside world—conflict with others, facing hardships without fear. This belief helped outwardly. But when things were in chaos inside me, I asked myself, *"What do I resort to?"*

"What kind of courage is needed now?"

Embracing Vulnerability as Strength

I began to question my own notion of this highly revered quality- courage. During one of the discourses, I heard that the word itself had **'rage'** hidden within it. This was quite a revelation inside me! Perhaps, too much courage had created a cycle of continuous rage against my own inner self and created unrest in the inner world.

For long, I had dodged the inner voice—the whispers, the unrest—that wanted to see light. The toughest of emotions need expression- else it leads to suffocation within. But I had no outlet to release these emotions. As a result, they continued to manifest as pains and aches in my body, sometime emotional breakdowns.

What I did not learn to express, my body chose to manifest- I had to embrace this truth!

Throughout my healing journey, I realised that my conditioning had taught me to cry in silence, feel sadness in the corners of my soul, and suppress my feelings for the "greater good"—sometimes for family, or to maintain peace in a given situation. Once or twice, this might be okay, but living and growing with this pattern over the years can definitely lead to disaster, even chronic auto-immune diseases.

Dr. Gabor Maté, the author of the book 'When the body says No' has noted that women are disproportionately affected by autoimmune diseases, accounting for approximately 80% of the cases. Societal expectations and the stress of carrying emotional burdens, often resulting in the repression of anger and healthy self-expression are some major reasons for this condition. This, in turn, can impact the immune system and contribute to the development of autoimmune conditions.

An autoimmune condition is when the body's immune system starts attacking its own healthy cells and hence the dis-ease is created within. No external infection or so.

I wasn't aware of this fact until I myself experienced it, internally. It left me no choice but to work on my own body by paying attention and re-establishing its connection with the mind and the depths of my soul.

As I began to break these conditioned patterns and create new ways of thinking, I learned to embrace **my own vulnerabilities**. It meant there was no hiding, no sidelining my feelings—just the simple act of being okay with feeling pain, acknowledging this pain, grieving it, and noticing how it was affecting me and my relationships.

This new learning also exposed a side of my personality that never wanted to appear weak or meek. I had learned to put on a face, ignore the difficult stuff, suppress tough emotions, and smile. This approach worked in some situations, but not as a universal way to deal with life—especially not in relationships at home or at work even.

If I'm not okay feeling sad, how will the other person ever get an opportunity to help me deal with it?

How would they know that their behavior impacts me?

Going back to the word **"courage,"** it finally started to make sense when I reframed it as:

"With courage, I choose to be vulnerable."

How does that sound to you?

Does it feel doable?

This new thought about courage with vulnerability, shifted my feelings and actions. My relationship with myself improved. It in fact created a ripple effect—bringing beauty into my relationship with the world.

I could manage conflicts with confidence and find strength in being vulnerable. I learned to process my pain and allow myself to feel it—without trying to stop, avoid, or ignore it.

Like an observer, I began to witness these waves of emotion and allowed them to settle on their own—without judgement or analysis. This presence brought awareness about my own thoughts, feelings, expectations, beliefs and behavior.

How does 'courage and vulnerability' show up in your life?

Learning to Ask for Help

One significant action that I embraced was **asking for help** whenever I needed it—instead of silently expecting others to just guess, know and offer. Trust me, learning to do this has been one of the most courageous acts for me.

Earlier, I used to wait and when my need wasn't met, I'd feel frustrated. As partners in a loving relationship, we often carry the weight of expectation without telling the other person:

"I want you to do this for me,"

or

"I feel burdened when you don't get up early with me to manage the household while we send the kids off to school. It leaves me feeling crazy—as if I'm battling it all alone in the mornings. I need your help."

If both partners are working, the dialogue could be:

"I also have to go to work. Let's do this together, so we're both sharing the load."

Say it, with kindness, before you erupt like a volcano. When you don't express, the other person is left guessing—and slowly starts accepting your eruptions as your "normal/abnormal/absurd" behavior. I have heard people label their loved ones as crazy, mad and demanding when they are angry etc. It happens because the other person doesn't know how to handle your outburst and then starts the trail of accusations, avoidance and rejections etc.

So, the learning is to learn to process your needs and wants and also communicate your expectations with care and this openness to embrace whatever emerges. Many of us have not learnt to listen to understand but all of us are conditioned to justify our position to be right. What's your experience?

Therefore, processing your want is an important step here. Stay patient as you are dealing with another human, who is conditioned differently. Be aware that you are on an inner journey of self-awareness which might not have begun for them yet.

Use your discretion, of course. But if you've done your inner work and are clear about what you need, how you need it, and then—chances are, you'll be perceived as a stronger, sharper, and more authentic individual. Clear articulation only happens when we move away from assumptions and accusations towards authenticity and camaraderie without fear of appearing weak or naïve.

The Role of Mindfulness in allowing Emotions Flow

Practicing mindfulness supports Emotional processing beautifully, I have experienced this magic myself.

Our emotions keep our human experience alive. They come in a broad range and are subtle chemical messages arising in the body as we move through life. My favorite analogy is that of a **river and its ripples**:

Life is like a beautiful river, flowing gently and silently.

Emotions are the ripples, caused by an event—either internal or external.

Sometimes the river turns or hits a rock or pebble, and a ripple is created. It's temporary, transitory, and yet—if you look closely—the beautiful process of flow for the river's journey to the ocean continues.

The river doesn't stop, it corrects its course and find ways to flow through forests, weathering storms and facing obstacles. It knows it's true nature: to keep going, embracing changes and ready for transformation.

If you've ever sat beside a river, try throwing a pebble in. Notice the circular ripples around the point where it lands in water. That's exactly how emotions work—spontaneous, short lived and beautiful. Strong emotions have the power to cause destruction and breaking, so learning to process and regulate these is the key for healthier living.

In this analogy, the forces of gravity and resistance are also present. These can represent our **intention** or **inner resistance**.

Ask yourself:

- Are you holding some tough emotions in your heart since a long time, refusing to let them release?
- Are you withdrawing, afraid of letting the world notice your feelings?
- Are you judging your own ripples created by your own emotions?
- Do you feel free to express yourself?

I love this parallel because it reminds me to learn from **nature and its elements**—the most vibrant, patient teacher of all. You just need to be willing to observe and be present to imbibe the learnings.

Practicing awareness and connection in Nature

Spending time in nature is **deeply therapeutic**

and some ways to engage in nature are-

Step into the sunlight

Breathe in the fresh air

Soak in the warmth of the morning sun

Touch the leaves, hug a tree

Smell the flowers, feel the earth

Walk barefoot on grass

Watch the night sky, the stars, the clouds

Hear the birds, the rustling leaves,

Witness the stillness of the night

All this is pure transformational magic, waiting for us! The best part is it happens each day, so start anytime you choose.

Pause and ask yourself:

- Am I *really* available?

- Am I present in this wonder that holds healing?
- Where am I giving my energy?
- What am I bringing back to myself?
- Who have I chosen to surround myself with?

Where your **attention flows**, your **awareness grows**. This leads to awareness on our actions and the subsequent results/ impacts that we see in our lives. Cultivating self-awareness is a skill, a process and a practice at the same time.

Practicing this awareness is the beginning of living with mindfulness leading us into a state of staying present with body, mind and soul-together always and every time.

Chapter 8

Healing Relationships – From Pain to Connection

"Genuine relationships depend first on a healthy relationship with ourselves."
— Sonia Choquette

How Brokenness Affects Our Relationships

Navigating relationships—with ourselves and with others—is one of the most fundamental, yet complex aspects of human life.

Ironically, we often enter relationships seeking love, harmony, and happiness. But in today's world, when we look around—at society, at families—we see many are living not in connection, but in quiet disconnection. We perform roles—spouse, siblings, parents, friends—often forgetting the emotional and psychological aspects involved in each of these relationships.

When we go inwards and shift our emotional state, we begin to change the vibrational field around us. Old patterns start to fall away. The stronger the emotion, the greater the energy it commands. The transformative process often brings chaos, initially and a lot of unpredictability before a new order emerges. But that's where the healing journey begins.

We start to acknowledge and realize:

'This isn't how I want to be in the world.

This isn't how I want to lead my life anymore.'

With this realization comes a wondering and a longing:

"What do I want my relationships and my life to look like, feel like, and sound like?"

Personally, this is where my life started to transform. If I am no longer wanting to be my previous self, with this new awareness, who do I want to be? – A gorgeous journey to embark!

The Echo Within

After a severe car crash and several triggering life events, I found myself exhausted—physically and emotionally. My patience had run dry. I felt burdened by expectations, real and perceived. But looking deeper, I realized I was struggling with setting healthy boundaries. I didn't know how to say "no." And I didn't have the emotional tools to deal with everything that surfaced.

I would often ask myself:

- *Why did I react that way?*
- *Could I have handled that without being so emotional?*
- *Why does the past keep spilling into the present?*

This is what happens to many couples, friends, and family members. A present-day trigger opens the floodgates to unresolved issues from the past. The conversation shifts from what is happening **now** to everything that has **ever** happened. The result? The current issue gets lost, and the pain deepens because of the past bitterness emerging back and diluting the present matter in hand. Instead, loads of unpleasant words, comments upon each other show up, which unintentionally cause more hurt and distasteful experience. So, to protect ourselves from all this, we tend to choose an approach of shutting down by not raising, talking or expressing real feelings at all.

What is your experience of a similar situation? Is this a relatable?

Deconstructing the Disconnect

Let's pause and examine what these moments typically look, sound, and feel like:

- **Looks like**: Picking fights, arguments, bringing up old stories irrelevant to the current moment.
- **Sounds like**: Yelling, blaming, justifying, ignoring, proving a point.

- **Feels like**: Dismissal, rejection, emotional overwhelm, unseen, unheard.
- **Results in**: Blame-shifting, emotional shutdown, misunderstanding.

All we want is to feel understood. But what prevails is miscommunication.

When we zoom out from the situation, we realize that feelings from past events keep showing up.

No one wanted to spoil the present. But **we did.**

And why so?

Because we didn't speak when we were hurt. We didn't share when things felt wrong. We shut down. We waited for someone to "get it" without us having to express it.

I've seen this play out in every kind of

relationship—between parents and children, spouses, colleagues, and friends. Silence becomes the norm in the name of love and understanding. But, in my case, it resulted into disconnection and emotional distancing because of always suppressing emotions. And slowly, this kind of love and understanding becomes serious resentment and an unwanted obligation to bear the load.

What If We Had...

Looking back, I wish I had:

- Initiated open, honest conversations
- Set boundaries—with love, not fear
- Trusted myself to navigate conflict
- Operated from love, not fear of rejection

Instead, I waited to be understood. I waited for

someone else to repair things. I kept my wounds quiet. And so, they stayed unhealed.

Today, I believe that **communication, conflict resolution, and emotional intelligence** are not just corporate skills—they are life skills not just for adults, but our children too.

Understanding the Relationship Dilemma

Wherever humans exist, relationships are formed. Their **quality**—good or bad—depends on what each of us brings to them.

"A relationship is the way two or more people are connected, or how they behave towards each other."

-Cambridge Dictionary

Yet generation after generation, we pass on the same confusion about relationships. Comedians mock the wedding dramas, "rishtedars" come with labels, and we all pretend like it's normal.

In my workshops with parents I hear them say, "There's a generation gap," "They need independence" or sometimes blame the "me-time culture" when children don't behave as expected.

But why don't we embrace that a generation gap will always exist?

We're not supposed to raise children while we are still children ourselves and are expected to work on our own inner child cravings and refrain from parenting in the way we were parented once. That context and time was different.

However, children always need love and peace to grow well and this fundamental human need always stay relevant for all times.

Let's explore a few modern phrases we often hear:

1. **"Generation Gap"** – It's not a gap, it's growth and part of the societal, contextual evolution and our adaptation to it.
2. **"Independence"** – Read again: *in-dependence.* It means we are connected in many ways that we often don't explore enough.
3. **"Me Time"** – It sounds liberating. But when not practiced mindfully, it creates emotional and mental separation. Now even children ask for "me time"—shutting doors and shutting out connection.

One of the reels on social media read a young mother sharing, "I need a break from my own children."

As a parent, educator and mindfulness coach, this breaks my heart.

These are **not signs of freedom**, but **symptoms of disconnection.**

The need of this mother is to find time to connect to her own self through support and guidance.

Reflection: What are you taking to your relationships?

1. What patterns from your childhood are playing out in your relationships?
2. Are you repeating behaviours that were never yours to begin with?
3. Do you carry unresolved expectations or wounds?

Our parents modelled what they could. They showed us resilience, kindness, and love in many ways. But they also had wounds. They, too, were raised in different times, with different tools. We must learn to honor their journey without glorifying and getting stuck in it. Just shift into a new reality with a new thought pattern that empowers you and others around you.

The Context of Change and Healing in relationships

The world around us is changing fast—socially, economically, technologically. But our **emotional literacy** hasn't kept up. The **inner world** needs more time to evolve.

This tug-of-war between outer change and inner resistance creates chaos in relationships. But healing starts by **asking better questions**.

The world is in a transformative phase and spiritual energy shift is emerging strongly. It is a great opportunity to begin your own healing journey.

Pause and Reflect

Dear reader, take a moment and reflect on a relationship you deeply care about:

- Are you holding assumptions about how it should be?
- Are your expectations helping or hurting the relationship?
- What do you want from this relationship?
- What are you giving to it?

If you notice stored pain, unspoken conflict, or habitual silence—it's time to make a shift.

Mere survival is not the goal but conscious thriving is.

Transformation is an inside-out journey. And

once we begin, we slowly start shifting every outer experience.

"The wound is the place where the Light enters you."

— Rumi

So, let's see our wounds as cracks—letting the light in. Let's rearrange our brokenness and realign ourselves with the wholeness we were born into.

Activity: Connect With the Pain

Many body pains and chronic illnesses are manifestations of held emotional pain and stress, as shared in the previous chapters.

Let's try this simple practice. Take a few minutes to:

Sit in a comfortable posture in silence. Take 3 cycles of deep breath and try noticing if you are feeling tight or heavy or strained anywhere in your body. Try connecting to that part and ask gently: *What pain am I storing here? What have I not spoken or expressed?*

Journal your thoughts, feelings, and what your body wants you to notice. Repeat as needed. Listen closely and just observe.

Reclaim, Repair, Reconnect

We always have a choice—to stay wounded, or become wiser.

Reclaim your whole self.
Embrace your brokenness.
And turn it into beauty.

Ask yourself if you are ready for this shift?

Are there any fears or apprehensions at this stage?

What might be some of your internal barriers to this process? Who can help you release?

Case Study 1

Anuya's Awakening – Healing the mother -daughter Bond

Anuya, a 39-year-old teacher and single mother, came to one of my emotional resilience workshops looking visibly exhausted. She had been struggling with a strained relationship with her teenage daughter, Meera. Their home was filled with arguments, silence, and a growing emotional distance. Anuya often found herself saying, *"She doesn't understand how much I do for her,"* while Meera often shut herself in her room, saying, *"You don't get me."*

During one of our journaling exercises, Anuya had a powerful realization: *she was repeating the same patterns her mother once used with her.* The emotional outbursts, the high expectations, the lack of space to just be—she had inherited these patterns without questioning their relevance in the present context.

What shifted everything was a single reflective prompt:

"What am I bringing to this relationship that is unresolved within me?"

Tears flowed as Anuya wrote about her own childhood—never feeling heard, always being expected to be "the good girl." She realized that her inability to hold space for her daughter's emotions was tied to how she was once denied that very space.

Over the next few weeks, she began changing her approach—not by fixing her daughter, but by healing herself with conscious effort and greater awareness.

She started:

- Practicing mindful pause and patience instead of reacting.
- Apologizing for past moments when she had dismissed Meera's feelings.
- Creating intentional moments of connection—a walk, a conversation, a shared meal without expectations or agenda.
- Naming her feelings and encouraging her daughter to do the same.

Slowly, over time, her daughter, Meera responded. She started opening up about school stress, friendships, and her dreams.

The yelling reduced. Laughter returned in their relationship.

Anuya's transformation wasn't dramatic or overnight—but it was real. She later shared "I thought I needed to fix my daughter. Turns out, I just needed to heal myself first."

Your own healing is a gift to your loved ones!

Reflection:

Anuya's story is not unique—it echoes in homes, classrooms, and relationships all around us. When we shift from blame to awareness, from control to curiosity, from pain to presence, we begin the true journey of healing ourselves especially the parts that need light.

Case Study 2

The Silence in the Hallways – An Urban Family with Everything

The Mehtas live in a plush 3BHK apartment in South Mumbai. From the outside, they seem to have it all—financial stability, international vacations, a house help team, a thriving business, and two children enrolled in the best IB school in the city.

But inside their tastefully done-up home, silence has become a default way of living.

Rahul, the 45-year-old father, works late hours and often unwinds with Netflix or late-night calls. He tells himself he's working for the family.

Ira, 42, a highly educated woman who left her career to raise the children, feels emotionally isolated. Her days revolve around managing the home, and her evenings revolve around managing her own emotional state.

Their children, Aarav (16) has stopped having meals with the family. Locked in his room, his world is filled with gaming and Instagram. Siya (13), once bubbly, now gets frequent stomach aches and prefers to be in bed scrolling reels.

They all love each other—but none of them feels loved.

In a family therapy session that Ira attended alone, she broke down.

"We have everything—but we feel like strangers living under one roof."

As we explored her story, deep patterns emerged—unspoken grief from a miscarriage 10 years ago, resentment at Rahul's emotional unavailability, guilt over not "doing enough" as a mother, and confusion about her own self-worth and self-identity.

When she was asked: **"What emotions are allowed to be expressed in your family?"**

She paused. "Only success. Everything else is seen as drama."

This one statement captured the culture of many modern families—where vulnerability is replaced by performance, and feelings are filtered through screens, salary packages etc.

The healing began not with a big family intervention, but with Ira beginning to feel connected to herself again.

- She began journaling her emotions every morning.

- She started expressing appreciation to her children and husband—not for what they did, but for who they were.
- She initiated "Tech-Free Sundays" for family connection. The first few were awkward. But by week three, they were playing Uno, cooking together, and even cracking jokes with their teenagers.

When Ira stopped pretending everything was perfect, the family stopped pretending too.

Are we okay admitting the silent cracks?

💡 Reflection:

In today's urban homes, **success often hides suffering**, and privilege often masks pain. When love becomes a checklist and communication is transactional, we begin to *survive in style* but forget to *live in connection.*

This case study reminds us that:

- Emotional wellness is not guaranteed by material wealth.
- Children don't need perfect parents—they need present ones.
- Healing begins when one person chooses to be real.

Even in homes with full fridges and fast Wi-Fi, emotional hunger can thrive.

But so can healing—when we choose it.

At this point pause for a moment and ask yourself- 'Am I ready to heal myself?'

✏️ Journaling & Reflection Prompt: Coming Home to Yourself

Take a few quiet moments today. Breathe. Then reflect on the following:

1. What emotions were allowed to be expressed freely in your childhood home? Which were suppressed or shamed?

2. What unspoken rules or expectations still influence how you show up in your relationships today?

3. In what ways have you prioritized performance over presence in your home or with your loved ones?

4. What would it feel like to be emotionally honest, just for a moment, with yourself or someone close to you?

5. What's one small, loving ritual you could begin this week—to reconnect, to listen, or to simply be together without distraction?

Healing doesn't always start with grand gestures. Sometimes, it begins with a single honest word, a deep breath, or a willingness to feel what you've long ignored.

The most powerful work we can do for our relationships is the work we do within ourselves, with ourselves and for ourselves.

I call this an act of authentic self-love and a deep service to our loved ones!

Case Study 3: The Silent Storm in Urban Homes

Ananya and Vikram, both professionals in their mid-30s, live in a beautiful high-rise apartment in Mumbai. Financially stable, they go for a vacation twice a year, send their child to an international school, and share Instagram reels of their 'perfect' life.

But behind closed doors, the authentic connection is missing.

Vikram often works late and zones out in front of the TV. Ananya, overwhelmed with parenting, work, and managing the home, feels unseen and unloved. They barely talk—except about logistics. Date nights are rare. Their child, Aarav, now 11, prefers being in his room with headphones on.

Despite therapy apps and YouTube videos,

both of them feel stuck.

The deeper truth?

Neither Ananya nor Vikram learned emotional expression while growing up. They were raised to achieve, not feel. Conflicts in their families were either suppressed or exploded into blame games. Today, both of them carry those same patterns.

As a conditioned response to a tough situation or in moments of conflict in relationships:

- Vikram shuts down.
- Ananya breaks down.
- Both retreat into silence or overwork.

They live in the same house. But emotionally? They're in different worlds.

Healing began when both of them joined a

mindfulness group. Slowly, they began journaling, sketching and drawing mandalas. They learnt to share their feelings vulnerably—first with self, then with each other. At first, they experienced resistance. But over time, sensing calmer presence and emotional clarity, both began to connect deeply.

It wasn't a perfect road. But it was real. They introduced simple rituals:

- No-phone at dinner time
- Daily "feelings check-in"
- Naming and validating their own emotions without judgement

Their relationship didn't need fixing.

It needed *feeling*.

What does your intimate relationship need at present?

Chapter 9

The Mind-Body Connection – Healing from the Inside Out

"Healing is a matter of time, but it is sometimes also a matter of opportunity." –*Hippocrates*

How Our Bodies Store emotional pain

Our body is like a container that holds and stores emotions as these are energies in movement. This body is our powerhouse, our sacred sanctuary. The soul resides in the body—it is the most holy place we inhabit.

It gives us form, shape, and structure to exist in this world. It is the tangible wealth we are all born with. It blesses us with sense organs to interact with the world and stay in sync with the world inside us.

For instance, if you think of a red rose—immediately, a thought or feeling associated with it kicks in. Any random memory of love, pain, grief, or beauty—whatever is inside—emerges.

What magic is happening here! It's just an automatic response to a picture or a thought of red rose.

For those who are deeply in sync with themselves, this rhythmic interaction between the inside and outside can even feel telepathic—like a common experience.

It is our body that makes this inner-outer

connection possible. Astonishingly, it's a wise container with the power to repair, regenerate, rejuvenate, and recharge itself. Without us even knowing or doing anything consciously, its systems interact with each other through chemicals (remember studying this in school science classes).

Amazing! Isn't it?

Think of the quality and speed of these interactions. The response we see outside is breathtaking. Faster than any AI in the world.

How marvelous it is to know that we are born with our own inherent AI systems, unique, personal and always available to us.

A Common Situation from Life:

Think of a child being scolded or denied something. How many milliseconds does it take for the child to weep or slump into a sad posture?

A simple tap of the foot or a door slammed shut communicates volumes. There's an exchange of information and a bodily response to that situation.

Now, reverse it.

Say you agreed to buy the child a toy. There is joy, chuckles, and excitement—even before the toy has been handed over. You can feel and see it in the child's face and body movements.

What is happening inside during this outside interaction? Do you notice a connection?

I remember when we studied the endocrine system, I marveled at how powerful it is. There's something strange just above the kidneys, usually dormant until activated by a trigger in the external environment—the adrenal glands. These produce adrenaline, preparing the body for a fight-or-flight response to stress or excitement.

I'm mindful that this doesn't turn into a revision of school biology class but I'm trying to highlight this fact that the body has its own emergency response mechanism.

Isn't this brilliance at work?

Let's understand this through an example: You're in a jungle, and a lion is approaching. Do you have time to plan a strategy? No.

The first and best response is to run! Your body takes over to save you. The danger—an emotion called fear—activates this reaction.

You might ask, what's the novelty here?

As we explore the mind-body connection, it is

essential to:

- Understand- how the body is designed to function.
- Recognize how physical awareness opens the door to mental and emotional awareness.

Without this, we end up repeating patterns and living in a way that ignores the body's signals and sensations—pains, fevers, racing heart, fluctuating blood pressure, etc.

Another profound perspective is to see the body as a system of systems—carefully designed, interdependent, and wholesome. It works 24x7, 365 days a year, as long as we live.

Until our death, this body is our only home. We experience everything in the outside world through it. It is our greatest wealth.

The key to all kinds of awareness starts with the

body. Listen to it. Sit with it.

If you are experiencing or have experienced painful moments of grief, frustration, or isolation—it's time to tune into your body.

Just Notice:

• How does someone's word impact me?

• How do I feel within?

•What is grief feeling like in my body at this moment?

• Am I scratching my own wounds by replaying that movie in my mind?

• If yes—ask, how is it helping?

• If no—go deep within. (This book reached you because somewhere, you were seeking for it.)

In my experience, when my seeking was true,

the solution found its way to me—perfectly in tune with that seeking.

Some call this manifestation.

Harmonious alignment of the 3 H

I like to think of it as a magical alignment of the 3H-head, heart, and hand—when thoughts, feelings, and actions move together in sync. The formula looks like:

Mind (thoughts) + Body(feeling) + Doing(action)—all in alignment and with clarity of direction.

That's where the empowerment lies. That's where transformation begins for the world to notice.

You can play with different combinations and approaches, but when these three come into harmony, they hold the power to shift the realities of your life.

When I add the other H (Healing) to the process, the attempt is to activate the connection between the mind and body. If there's disconnection or lack of alignment among the three, it creates painful realities. Being aware of your own 3H (Head, Heart, and Hand) is the key.

I experienced this in my own journey.

My mind constantly replayed past events, whispering: "You've been so brave for the sake of this relationship. You're courageous and kind, even when others are unkind. Stay true to your goodness. Stand tall. This will pass. Show the world your strength."

This internal dialogue went on for years. Painful moments piled up. I only focused on thoughts and action. Feelings were ignored.

Beware—your mind creates endless narratives to keep you safe. This can slowly lead to collapse, if the body is neglected for a longer time.

I never shied away from weeping. I questioned everything. But I was conditioned to mask my feelings. I thought no one cared. I had to be stronger. Braver. Bouncing back was my superpower.

As a result, my body was left behind. Days turned into weeks, months, and years. Pain and discomfort became constant.

My Coping Mechanisms were:

1. Read something inspiring and move on
2. Eat something sweet
3. Go for a walk
4. Sleep it off

5. Talk to a friend
6. Shop
7. Be with children
8. Cook something new

Doctor consultations and medications became part of my routine for over 15 years.

All these were temporary fixes. They worked briefly but eventually led to illness because I ignored my pain and denied my own unpleasant emotions and de-prioritized my emotional needs to feel safe, heard and valued.

I wasn't ready to appear weak.

I had responsibilities.

I was educated. I was earning. I was "doing my best."

This is what an ego-based self looks like:

constantly trying to be wise, right, and courageous while ignoring one's own deeper emotional needs.

Operating in the world for others isn't bad—if it fulfils you as well. If you feel inner peace and ease when you sit in silence, that's great. If in your body and mind, you feel good about yourself, that's wonderful.

But wait—this might just be your mind talking.

Check in with yourself:

• Have I taken my heart along in what I think and do?

•How does the Head, Heart and Hand alignment show up in my personal life?

You may struggle at first. Your ego may shield you from these questions. It will whisper: "You're doing fine. Better than most. Look at your life—good education, job, family, comfort. What more do you need?"

Time to Reflect:

- What does real success mean to me?

- What do I truly need in my life right now?

- Is there something unknown that whispers to me but I've missed? How does that make me feel?

If you're someone who values both wealth and wonder, and inner harmony feels essential—this is your invitation to go within.

Layer by layer with curiosity and compassion.

Connect back to the body—it always lives in the present. It whispers. Start listening.

Listen:

- Without judgment

- Without doubt
- Not to respond, but to understand
- With love and care

If your body feels heavy, aching, or sick—see it as a wake-up call. Attend to it. Rest and relax as needed.

Practice body-centric awareness each day.

Collect information on:

- What needs to be processed within you and in your life? How?

Remember that each journey is personal.

Tailor it to your own needs.

Bea ready to learn from your own life and respect this journey as your guiding light—navigate your path with love, care, gentleness, and generosity.

When your life experience at individual level improves, it has a ripple effect on your relationships.

My personal experience of healing through embodiment.

We are all part of a larger construct. This way Healing begins with self and expands to those around us. It cannot be contained. It alleviates others' suffering. It's a gift you give to yourself first—then extend to others through your mindful and loving presence.

It starts with self-awareness, leading to people-awareness extending towards planet awareness.

Considering the weather crises and conflicts arising in the world, many healers believe in the work of planet consciousness because we are part of this lovely planet. So, we can't see ourselves any different from it.

I want us to think of well-being as an interconnected and integrated, wholesome idea that brings us all together to ourselves and others. Here is a little visual to help us practice and extend awareness for a larger good. Observe the 9 practices and notice the connection:

Self-awareness		People awareness		Planet awareness
1. Breathwork {to align mind and body}	⟷	4. Practice letting go	⟷	7. Connect with Nature
2. Movement {to create space}	⟷	5. Choose calm & connection	⟷	8. Appreciate interdependence
3. Mindfulness {to cherish the present}	⟷	6. Practice forgiveness & listening more	⟷	9. Acknowledge Oneness & Take Action

Start seeing yourself as energy in this cosmos. The energy each of us holds has the power to transform not just ourselves, but the world. It expands into collective consciousness, starting from within.

You don't need to find it outside. Be open to discovering it within.

To shift your outer experience, go within.

Hold this image in your heart—believe that you are part of a greater force holding us all together.

Trust and be resilient about the change that only *you* can bring to this world.

After all, your presence here must find its purpose—for a richer, more meaningful, extraordinary life.

Remember: *"I become what I choose to be."*

PART 4

We may not be responsible for the way the world creates our mind, but we can learn to take responsibility for the mind with which we create our world.

- Dr. Gabor Mate

Celebrating your whole self

Chapter 10

Wounds to Wisdom

"The world breaks everyone and afterward many are strong at the broken places."

— Ernest Hemingway

Transforming brokenness into beauty

To transform is to heal and to heal is to recognise our inherent wholeness and completion as a form of life on this miraculous planet. As shared earlier, we have a choice to stay wounded and lament- Why did life break me open?

Or, to practice wisdom and ask ourselves:

How do I rearrange my brokenness into something of beauty and grace? (this unlocks doors to a newer possibility, as it did for me)

I feel thankful towards my pains and wounds as there were hidden lessons for me to discover and learn about myself. Such profound learnings emerge not out of joys but through our pains- deep, intense moments which break us open to shift our perspectives and re-direct us.

My views, of life as a continuous struggle and myself as a 'warrior' created more breaking for me. But the shift began when I learnt to embrace my pains; my entire perception shifted and I now see pains as a cry for help and attention, so tend to these in time without blame but full ownership.

It could be that these pains are emerging from a feeling of disconnection, or unwanted relationships, expectations. Re-connection and restoration of love is a sustainable solution.

Pain is an invitation and wounds are gateways because physical pains and injuries are challenging but can lead to tremendous growth. Such experiences can be seen as a catalyst for personal transformation. Not all change is transformation but all transformation encompasses a series of internal shifts and change. Think about it.

Pain is inevitable but suffering is a choice-sharing this wisdom in the form of a self-composed poem-

It might be the pain of rejection,
which is a deep cry for a compassionate action,
It might be pain of failure or loss,
which indicates a need to sit back and pause.

It might be the pains of the past still living in your mind,
with gentleness and love, let's choose to unwind
For pain is an opportunity to practice grace
but we have made our lives an unending race.

That hasn't helped us feel enough,
but has made us think that life is tough,
In essence, Life is simple and full of love-
failures and obstacles are not to shove.

Let us embrace every aspect of our lives
Realize that it is we, who have to make a choice!

My dear reader, let me remind you that have your own treasures of wisdom waiting to be reached within your own heart. Therefore, the intention is to take it along and keep it close in your view so that whenever you go and whatever you do, you don't forget to take your heart with you. (Remember the 3 H- Head, Heart and Hand)

I have embraced struggles as a part of my life each day. I thank these struggles which if would not have been there- I would not have been able to create and live this present reality.

The newer realities are beautiful and this has expanded my capacity to look at life events as inherent milestones in the journey.

- Now I resist less and embrace more to think-What is it that I need to pay attention to?
- Is there anything for me to explore or to learn about myself or life?

I invite you to sit with yourself and ask yourself-

1.What new realities you want to live?

2. What inner shifts you want in your life?

3. Which are the areas in your life that you need to pay more attention? Is it career, money, relationships, spirituality, family, health?

4. Are you ready to turn your pain into power?

Turning Pain into Power: Tools for Inner Transformation

As mentioned earlier that this journey begins with awareness. Take a moment to sit with yourself, and gently ask:

What within me is calling for attention, for love, for a shift?

In addition to the mind-map shared earlier, here are some practices that supported me—and may support you too:

🌸 **Self-Compassion Check-ins**

💗 **Loving-Kindness Meditation**

🎵 **Healing Frequencies & Sound Baths**

💃 **Movement and Dance Therapy**

🌳 **Art: Mandala making**

🌸 **Mindful eating**

✍️ **Gratitude Journaling**

🧘 **Meditation & Breathwork**

🏃 **Daily Exercise**

🌟 **Reframing Beliefs Through NLP**

✨ **Tapping into my consciousness**

Some of the action steps that you can start with are detailed here:

1. **Own Your Story and Redefine Courage**

True healing begins when you stop being at war with yourself. Start owning all parts of you. Is it hard at first? Be patient.

For the longest time, I didn't realize how much of my energy was being spent on hiding my pain, fixing others, pleasing people, and avoiding difficult conversations—all in the name of being 'strong', 'calm', or 'spiritual.'

But spirituality isn't bypassing your pain—it's moving through it, being with it.

It's about holding space for your discomfort, sitting with your shadow, and listening to the stories your body wants to tell. It's about being so honest with yourself that even the truth you've been running away from feels like home.

Start telling yourself, "I am good wherever I am in my life."

---

2. **Remind yourself to honour your body- *it never lies***

When I couldn't say out loud what I truly

needed, my body found ways to speak for me—through fatigue, inflammation, brain fog, migraines, anxiety, irritation

It was my body's way of saying:

"You've carried enough. Please rest."

"Your truth is safe with me."

"You're allowed to feel and fall apart."

Instead of viewing my emotions or body symptoms as a weakness, I started seeing them as sacred messengers.

The body is not a battleground; it's a wise companion.

And this wisdom whispered to me: "You don't have to be perfect to be loved. You just have to be real."

---

3. Give yourself Permission to Feel

We all have moments when we're tired of being the strong one. The one who holds it together. The one who always shows up.

But what if *showing up* sometimes looks like crying in your car, asking for space, saying no, or cancelling plans?

What if true strength is in allowing yourself to be seen in all your humaneness?

That's what vulnerability is—*the courage to feel everything. No holding back.*

And it's not about being emotional all the time. It's about *being emotionally honest.*

Letting your guards down doesn't make you weak.

It makes you **Accessible. Authentic. Whole.**

---

4. Build Emotional Resilience

Emotional resilience isn't about bouncing back with a smile every time. It's about feeling deeply and still finding your way through with your kindness and love.

It's the ability to say:

- "These hurts, and I'm still here."
- "I'm scared, and I will take the next step."
- "I feel lost, but I trust that the path will reveal itself."

Over time, I realized that my emotions didn't need to be "managed." They needed to be *met* with attention.

Met with compassion.
With presence.
With breath.

With space.

---

5. Practices That Held Me

Here are a few other practices that supported me in building emotional resilience and embracing vulnerability as strength:

1. Name it to Tame it

Whenever you feel overwhelmed, pause and simply name the emotion that you are feeling:

"I feel sad."

"I feel unheard."

"I feel disconnected."

The simple act of naming brings clarity and softens the inner chaos.

2. Journaling Without Censoring

Start giving yourself the permission to write

your thoughts and feelings without any structure. No grammar. No coherence. Just raw emotion.

This prevents us from judging our own expression.

Often, I'd start with:

"I don't know what I'm feeling, but I need to write…"
and by the end, I had discovered something deeper.

3. Body Check-ins

Place a hand on your chest or belly and ask:

"What do you need right now?"

"Is there something I'm not listening to?"

The body always answers through sensations—gently, silently feel them. Stay with them.

4. Compassionate Inner Dialogue

Instead of pushing yourself to "get over it," begin asking:

"What would I say to a child feeling this?"

And then say that to yourself.

Stop being harsh and start being gentle with yourself. Become your inner ally and not a critic.

The world has enough critics already.

Write these affirmations by hand and keep them on your table or paste near a mirror to read and remind yourself each morning.

I am allowed

I am allowed to break down and still be brilliant.
I am allowed to ask for help and still be whole.

I am allowed to feel deeply and still be strong.
I am allowed to not have it all together.

There is a softness that lives inside my strength.
There is a warrior in my tenderness.

And when I choose to feel everything—
to be honest, raw, and present—
I don't lose myself.
I gently come home to yourself.

A Final Whisper

If you've been holding back your tears, your truth, your needs, remember

You were never meant to carry it all alone.
You were meant to feel, to connect, to heal.

And in that healing,
you become more you.

That is courage. That is love.
That is wholeness.

Invitation to check in: Coming Home to Yourself each night

Take a quiet moment, perhaps with a warm cup of tea, soft lighting, or calming music.

Sit with yourself—just as you are.

No fixing. No performing. No expectations.

Breathe.
Let your shoulders drop.
And ask yourself:

1. What am I feeling right now?
2. Where do I sense this feeling in my body?
3. What is this feeling trying to tell me?
4. What does it look like to offer myself compassion in this moment?

Now open your journal and complete this sentence: Today, I give myself permission to…

Write freely. Let the words spill. There are no right or wrong answers—only truth.

You might end your writing with a loving affirmation like:

"I am safe to feel. I am worthy of love, especially from myself."

Slowly you would be able to tweak your affirmations as you feel the need for it. This would indicate some progress for you.

Chapter 11

The beauty of brokenness- A new beginning

We humans are fragile; susceptible to breaks and knocks

Discover how to pick up the pieces and repair what may have been damaged in your life

Find out how to embrace your emotional scars and make them beautiful

They are proof that you have suffered…

- ***Thomas Navarro***

Scars are marks of efforts and maturity.

There is an embedded message of glory and grace waiting to unearth within our grief and agony.

Are you living fully even with scars?

When we become kinder to ourselves, we become kinder to the world, and

When we care for ourselves, the world will find us worthy of care.

The image of the broken heart that you see on the cover page invited you to this reading. How ordinary will it be without those golden nerves? This is inspired from an art form which we are about to explore.

Kintsugi: Beauty in the Broken

In Japan, there is a centuries-old art called **Kintsugi**. It is practice of repairing broken pottery with gold lacquer. The interesting aspect is that instead of hiding the cracks or fixing them, Kintsugi invites us to highlight them. This process makes the broken object even more beautiful and unique than before.

There isn't grief in the breaking but an opportunity in waiting. To be self-anew!

The word **Kintsugi** refers to 'golden repair'. It embraces the idea that imperfections are a part of an object's beauty. In essence, brokenness enhances the beauty. It helps in forming new identities and discovering different ways to be beautifully broken.

Aging is one such time in our lives when we must learn to embrace the beauty of life. It is not bad or to be running away from but to welcome as mark of our living on this planet. It is just a stage of life, embrace it and shine through it.

Wabi-sabi, is another Japanese concept that

inspires us to accept imperfection, impermanence, and incompleteness as life itself is transient in nature. Embrace simplicity and accept that physical flaws or changes are just a part of this human life.

Kintsugi as a Metaphor for Emotional Healing

Just like pottery, we too fall, shatter, and break. Life's challenges chip away at us. Trauma, grief, illness, heartbreak—these are the forces that crack our sense of self. But just as a Kintsugi artist tenderly gathers each broken piece and begins the slow process of mending with care, so we can also approach our healing and repair.

Be aware that Kintsugi is not about erasing the damage.

It's about honoring the story that the cracks are telling proudly.

Each crack becomes a vein of gold—an offering of wisdom, resilience, and grace. Instead of seeing ourselves as ruined or flawed, we begin to see the places we've been broken as the very places we've been *reborn* and illuminate from within.

Let's understand a parallel between emotional healing and transformation with the 4 steps of Kintsugi art:

1. **Gathering the Pieces**

We start by acknowledging what's broken within us. Our pain, our loss, our wounds and then decide to face our own darkness, without blame but with an intention to rediscover ourselves.

2. **Preparing the Surface**

With healing practices, we learn to let go of old beliefs, filters, and defense mechanisms that no longer serve us in maintaining peace and harmony in our lives.

3. **Joining with Gold**

The gold here is compassion, mindfulness, love, therapy, breathwork, or creative expression that helps us fill into the cracks of our soul to which the body responds.

4. **Polishing the Repaired Form**

We learn to integrate our experiences, emotions and emerge with deeper wisdom, softer strength, and radiant authenticity. This is the glow and glory stage.

All the past drama is gone and a new form has emerged from inside out.

We find our light that has the power to illuminate the world now.

The Kintsugi art reminds us that we are not

meant to stay shattered—we are meant to shine and expand this consciousness.

The process of healing takes patience, presence, and surrender with faith. Often, the parts we try the hardest to hide, hold our greatest light. Are you ready to trace your light?

Remember, when we honor our wounds, we inspire others to do the same and live in harmony with life.

Kintsugi is not just about the external beauty. It's a sacred philosophy.

This reminds us that -

We are worthy of love, even when we feel broken. We don't need to be perfect to be beautiful. Our healing is an art and science at the same time.

Interestingly, neuroscience also echoes this idea. Our brains are not fixed—they're wired to heal and grow. Through **neuroplasticity**, we can literally rewire our brains by creating new patterns of thoughts, practicing new habits, and adopting new behaviors.

Closing Reflection:

Embrace Your Golden Cracks

"Scars are not injuries… a scar is a healing. After injury, a scar is what makes you whole."

— China Miéville

You, dear reader, are a masterpiece. Each scar you carry is a story worth exploring and sharing.

Every painful experience, when met with love, can become a source of light.

So, let your cracks gleam with gold to lead you write a story of inner expansion. Not one of shame, but one of survival. One of spirit. One of strength.

You are not ruined, broken or buried.

You are *redesigned* to reclaim your own glory and grace in this world.

Self-work is a continuous journey and this doesn't end here, rather it has initiated within you.

Let the exploration continue…

"Our cracks become our crowning glory.

Our flaws, the place where love pours in."

— From *The Beauty of Brokenness*

An Invitation to Embrace Yourself fully

🌸 Affirmation Card: Kintsugi Healing 🌸

Read these aloud, daily, or during your quiet moments of reflection.

✨ I honour my brokenness—it is where my light enters.

✨ I am not defined by what happened to me, but by how I choose to heal.

✨ Every crack in my life has made me wiser, softer, and stronger.

✨ I give myself permission to shine—especially in the places I once hid.

✨ My healing is an art form, and I am the artist of my own wholeness.

✨ I celebrate my scars—they are golden threads of resilience.

🧘 "I am a beautiful, imperfect masterpiece in progress."

📝 **Journal Prompts for a deep dive:**

Reflective Writing for Integration & Inner Dialogue

1. What cracks or emotional wounds in your life do you tend to hide or avoid? What might change if you looked at them through the lens of Kintsugi?
2. Describe a time you felt broken. What did that experience teach you about yourself?
3. What parts of you are still healing? How can you offer them compassion instead of judgement?

4. If your soul were a piece of Kintsugi pottery, what golden wisdom would your scars hold? Write a love letter to yourself from your future healed self.

5. What "gold" have you discovered in your healing journey so far—strengths, insights, or transformations you didn't have before?

6. How would your life feel if you fully embraced your imperfections as gifts instead of flaws?

A letter to my readers

My dear friend,

If you've made it to this point, I want you to pause for a moment. Take a deep breath. Feel your heart beating, your body here in this present moment. You have walked through every word of this book, not just reading, but *feeling, questioning, reflecting with me.* That takes courage. And I want to tell you something from the depths of my heart—**I see you. I honour you. I am walking this journey with you.**

I know what it feels like to be shattered. I have lived through days when the weight of pain felt unbearable, when I questioned if I would ever feel whole again. There were moments when I lost sight of myself in the chaos of expectations, illness, heartbreak, and self-doubt. But here's what I discovered—

brokenness is not the end of our story rather it is the beginning of something beautiful.

Healing isn't an instant process and for me, it was a slow unfolding, a process of choosing myself, again and again. Of learning to listen to my emotions instead of running from them. Of letting go of beliefs that no longer served me. Of allowing love—not just from others, but from within—to soften the hard edges of my pain.

And as I healed, my relationships transformed. I began to connect with my children, my family, my friends—not from a place of fear or obligation, but from a space of deep love and presence. I started *living fully* instead of merely existing. And that has been the greatest gift of all.

"The present moment is the only time over which we have dominion." — Thich Nhat Hanh

This moment—right here, right now—is your

gift. No matter what has happened in the past or what uncertainties the future holds, *this moment* is yours to breathe, to love, to heal.

So, if you ever doubt your strength, remember this:

- You are not broken; you are becoming.
- You are not lost; you are finding your way home to yourself.
- You are not alone; you are held in love and understanding.

Healing is not about erasing the past. It is about holding it with tenderness and gratitude, knowing that it has shaped the resilient, wise, and deeply feeling person, you are today.

My journey brought me here—to a place where I can love and accept myself fully, where I can share my truth with you. And now, my deepest hope is that *you* find the courage to embrace yourself, scars and cracks, and step into the love and wholeness that has been waiting for you all along.

With love and grace

Shveta

ABOUT THE AUTHOR

Shveta Kapur is a certified Mindfulness and Wellbeing Coach, NLP Practitioner, Educational Consultant, Researcher and Master Trainer in Social Emotional Learning. A former educator with over two decades of experience working with children, teachers and parents, she now helps her clients heal, grow, and thrive from a place of inner alignment and abundance.

A recipient of the Triple Wellbeing Fellowship, her initiatives include wellbeing programs, workshops and the podcast *Mindfulness and Me,* promoting healthy relationships with self and others. Her guiding motto is 'I become what I choose to be.'

Connect on socials to explore her programs and workshops. Write to her at – smk.author25@gmail.com. Any questions, suggestions, feedback, testimonials are welcomed.